SAGE CONTEMPORARY SOCIAL SCIENCE ISSUES 46

SURVEY DESIGN AND ANALYSIS

Current Issues

Edited by

Duane F. Alwin

SAGE PUBLICATIONS   *Beverly Hills / London* 1978

301
Sue7
120484 - replacement
February 1982

The material in this publication originally appeared as a special issue of
SOCIOLOGICAL METHODS & RESEARCH (Volume 6, Number 2,
November 1977). The Publisher would like to acknowledge the assistance
of the journal's editors, George W. Bohrnstedt and Edgar F. Borgatta, and
the special issue editor, Duane F. Alwin.

For information address:

SAGE Publications, Inc.
275 South Beverly Drive
Beverly Hills, California 90212

SAGE Publications Ltd
28 Banner Street
London EC1Y 8QE

Printed in the United States of America
International Standard Book Number 0-8039-1021-5
Library of Congress Catalog Card Number 77-95433

THIRD PRINTING, 1982

CONTENTS

**SURVEY DESIGN
AND ANALYSIS**

This paper introduces the collection of papers in the present issue of Sociological
Methods and Research. *A framework is developed for considering issues in
survey methodology, especially those concerned with "errors in surveys," and an
overview of research in the area is presented. The paper emphasizes both the
concern with improving the quality of survey data in their collection and the
concern with improving the quality of the inferences made from survey data
in their analysis. A range of topics is covered, including discussions of completion
rates, sample coverage, locating respondents in longitudinal research, response
rates, item nonresponse, weighting to adjust for noncoverage and nonresponse
bias, interviewer variability, question structure and sequence, methods of administration, and respondent errors. The papers included in the present collection
focus on many of these issues and reflect the contemporary concerns of social
scientists with the problems of making errors using survey data.*

MAKING ERRORS IN SURVEYS
An Overview

DUANE F. ALWIN
Indiana University

S ample surveys have become a major source of data for studying
human social behavior. Sociologists have increasingly relied on
surveys as a data source for both theoretical and policy-oriented research (see Sudman, 1976b: 108). Large-scale survey organizations,
both governmental and private, have not only become a source of data
for sociological analysis, but have also become models for much
sociological research of smaller scale. The Current Population Survey
conducted by the United States Bureau of the Census, the National
Health Survey carried out by the National Center for Health Statistics,
surveys conducted by the National Opinion Research Center, and the
University of Michigan's Survey Research Center, among others, have
become exemplars for the design of sampling frames, the training and
management of interviewers, question and interview schedule design,
methods of improving completion rates, and procedures for handling
biases due to nonresponse.

AUTHOR'S NOTE: *The author wishes to thank Susan Stephens, J. Michael
Armer, and Howard Schuman for helpful comments on an earlier draft of this
paper.*

Historically, sociologists have shown a concern with making errors in surveys, a concern shared with other social scientists, market researchers, and pollsters. The large-scale survey organizations mentioned at the outset have led the way in devising strategies for minimizing errors which can occur in surveys, and a number of early reviews of errors in surveys by workers associated with these organizations are still useful (e.g., Deming, 1944; Hansen et al., 1951). The literature on survey methods has since become voluminous (see U.S. Census Bureau, 1974b).

Discussions of errors in surveys may focus on one (or both) of two kinds of tasks which the survey researcher faces. The first involves reducing errors at the data collection stage. Here the concern is with improving the quality of the data collected, either through improved theoretical and conceptual formulations of the problem or through improved methods of sampling, asking questions, interviewing, and so forth. The second set of tasks involves the analysis of already collected survey data which is known to have imperfections. Here the issues involve the possibilities of adjusting the data in some way in their analysis so as to compensate for errors which have crept in during their collection.

No matter how sophisticated one's analytic tools, the quality of one's inferences is intimately tied to the quality of the data. Those who have engaged in the collection of data through sample surveys know that it is a costly and time-engaging enterprise. Decisions which affect the ultimate quality of the survey data are often governed by practical considerations rather than theoretical and/or methodological ones. Issues of cost and efficiency, goals which the researcher himself may not wish to maximize (or minimize), influence the size of the sample, the kind and number of questions which may be included, and so on. In dealing with human populations, issues of ethics may also influence the eventual quality of one's data (Frankel, 1975). The fact, however, that practical considerations place limitations on the quality of the data does not provide a refuge to those who would ignore potential errors once they have been made. *It is untenable to confront survey data as if they were error-free.* There is no substitute to the careful approach to survey data, mending flaws where they are known and examining possible models for errors where they are essentially unknown.

This issue of *Sociological Methods and Research* reflects the contemporary concern of sociologists with the problems of errors in surveys. We conceive of errors in broad terms, and the papers included here represent the concerns with both improving the quality of data in their collection and improving the quality of inferences made from the data in their analysis. The purpose of this overview paper is to provide an outline for considering errors in surveys and a review of pertinent literature dealing with such errors. In developing this outline we have not attempted a laundry list of errors which can be made in survey research. Rather, we have concentrated on general sources of error which occur as one moves from the designation of a population and selection of a sample, through data collection, to the analysis of data. Nor, have we attempted an encyclopedic review of the available literature. Our citation of research on errors in surveys is guided by the importance of the problem as well as the representativeness of the research. Where possible, we have tried to draw attention to review papers when they exist. Our discussion is organized around the following outline:

(1) Population and Samples
(2) Sample Bias
    (a) Completion rates in surveys
    (b) Sample coverage
    (c) Locating respondents in longitudinal research
    (d) Response rates
    (e) Item nonresponse
    (f) Weighting to adjust noncoverage and nonresponse bias
(3) Response Errors
    (a) Interviewer variability
    (b) Question structure and sequence
    (c) Method of administration
    (d) Respondent errors

POPULATION AND SAMPLES

The statistician's distinction between population and sample is one which is well appreciated among survey researchers (see Kish, 1965; Sudman, 1976a). When the statistical conception of a population coincides with other conceptions, e.g., the demographer's (Ryder, 1964), analysis of samples becomes of substantive interest. By contrast, the popular image of the "general public" is not necessarily coincident with a population in the statistician's (or the demographer's) sense. We refer to subsets of a population generated by known probability processes as "samples," and subsets of a population generated by unknown processes as "nonsamples." Although there are uses to which nonsamples may be put (see Sudman, 1976a), clearly, they should be treated with caution in terms of representing populations of interest.

There are a number of problems with the sampling frames used to sample the populations studied by survey researchers. For example, when households are sampled, it is sometimes difficult to understand inferences regarding the behavior of populations of individuals, unless the procedures are adjusted to take differences in household composition into account (see Kish, 1949; Troldahl and Carter, 1964). Or, when telephone subscribers are used as the sampling frame, the possibilities of an unrepresentative sample exist. The U.S. Census Bureau (1976: 533) estimates that 95% of the population of households reports owning a telephone, but unlisted subscribers pose a problem of unknown proportion. Several studies (Perry, 1968; Leuthold and Scheele, 1971; Brunner and Brunner, 1971; Glasser and Metzger, 1975) indicate that the use of telephone listings to define a population under-represents important segments of the U. S. population, e.g., nonwhites, low income groups, residents of major metropolitan areas. The use of random digit dialing (Cooper, 1964; Hauck and Cox, 1974; Groves, 1977) or some combination of this with other methods (Sudman, 1973) will improve the representation of subscribers, but nonsubscribers are still excluded. [See Sudman (1976a) for an excellent discussion of the use of these methods.]

SAMPLE BIAS

Sample data used in social research may be different from the population sampled, producing differences between the parameters of the population and sample statistics. Sampling statisticians (e.g., Kish, 1965; U.S. Bureau of the Census, 1974a) make a distinction between random and nonrandom sources of these differences. Random differences are typically discussed under the heading of "sampling errors" and are dealt with using the tools of statistical inference. Nonrandom differences are referred to as "nonsampling errors" or "sampling bias," and are less manageable using available statistical theory. Here we outline three well-known potential sources of sampling bias related to the methods of survey research—sample coverage, response rates, and item nonresponse—and we discuss methods proposed for weighting data to adjust for sample bias.

Completion rates in surveys. Before discussing these sources of bias, we should clarify the terminology used. The "Report of the American Statistical Association Conference on Surveys of Human Populations" (American Statistical Association, 1974) emphasizes the need to develop uniform definitions of "completion rates, nonresponse, refusals, etc." Following the practice of the U.S. Bureau of the Census, we refer to the overall *completion rate* of a survey as the total sample minus all uncompleted interviews (regardless of cause) divided by the total sample. Our discussion of *sample coverage* (below) uses the term "noncoverage" to refer to uncompleted interviews which result from the inability of the survey organization to locate the sample elements or to find them at home. Our discussion of *response rates* (below) uses the term "nonresponse" to refer to uncompleted interviews from among the covered (or contacted) sample elements. The completion rate is then a function of both sample coverage and response rate.[1]

There has been some concern expressed that public acceptance of surveys has declined, resulting in lower overall completion rates (Business Week, 1973). This has not universally been the case. Governmental organizations that routinely conduct sample surveys of the U. S. population, such as the U. S. Bureau of the Census, report very high completion rates (usually above 90%). Lack of coverage accounts for most of the departure from total completion. By contrast, private survey organizations report much lower completion rates (from 60% to 80%), the departures from total completion resulting about equally from noncoverage and nonresponse (American Statistical Association, 1974; see also Sudman, 1976b). In the latter case, this represents an apparent decline over the experience in earlier decades, and this is the major source of concern about the public acceptance of surveys. The ASA Conference on Surveys of Human Populations concludes that while survey research appears to be in increasing difficulty, "little hard data are available for evaluating changing acceptance by respondents." (American Statistical Association, 1974: 30).

Sample coverage. There are obvious practical difficulties in obtaining contact with every sample element, and all members of a sample are rarely if ever reached. Individuals may not be at home, they may be unlocatable, they may be unable to respond, or they may refuse to respond (see below). For many of these same reasons, even complete censuses are difficult to obtain. The U.S. Census Bureau estimates that it has excluded part of the population in decennial censuses, e.g., 2.4% in 1950, 1.9% in 1960 (Taeuber and Hansen, 1964), and 2.5% in 1970 (Siegel, 1974). Depending upon the design of the research, sample coverage is usually much worse than this. Although rules of thumb are often given for an acceptable coverage rate, any departure from nearly full sample coverage is technically unacceptable. For this reason survey methodologists present procedures for reducing the noncovered portion of the sample to a minimum. The nearly universally accepted contact-seeking device among survey researchers is the use of repeated callbacks (or mailbacks).

A number of studies employing wave analysis have attempted to quantify the amount of bias resulting from noncoverage in the absence of repeated callbacks and the gains associated with each successive call (see Sharp and Feldt, 1959; Schwirian and Blaine, 1966-1967; Dunkelberg and Day, 1973; Hawkins, 1975). Such research provides a sound basis for determining the cost-effectiveness of a callback effort. The paper in this issue by Gideon Vigderhous, "Patterns of Response to Mailed Questionnaires," shows that the patterns of response to mail surveys may be described by the Gamma distribution. His discussion points out how this knowledge may be used to forecast the response patterns in mail surveys.

The major principle governing the handling of sample coverage is that the noncovered portion of the sample must either be held to an absolute minimum, or measures must be taken to correct for the resulting bias. Daniel (1975) reviews several methods which have been proposed in the methodological and statistical literature to overcome bias due to noncoverage and/or adjust data to obtain better estimates of population parameters.

Locating respondents in longitudinal research. A unique set of issues regarding sample coverage is involved in research utilizing panels or in longitudinal studies in which a follow-up of the original sample is carried out. *Sample attrition* becomes a potential source of bias (see Williams, 1970), but in contrast to the cross-sectional survey, information is available in such research for investigating the nature and sources of bias. A number of papers in the literature describe techniques for successfully locating mobile respondents. Eckland's (1968) paper indicates that these devices are often more a part of folklore than of the standard repertoire of the survey researcher. Eckland argues, in any case, that "most of these [mobile] cases *can* be retrieved, and if a longitudinal study comes out badly, it usually is because little or no effort was made to do so" (1968: 53). Eckland reviews several accounts of successful attempts to minimize sample attrition in longitudinal surveys (e.g., Eckland, 1965; Sewell and Hauser, 1975). More recent efforts to retrieve mobile cases using the best available methods demonstrate that *very high sample coverage is possible* (see Crider et al., 1972; Crider and Willits, 1973; McAllister et al., 1973a, 1973b; Alwin and Jensen, 1976; Mortimer and Lorence, 1977; Clarridge et al., forthcoming). There are instances, however, when even the best methods fail to achieve a high level of coverage (see Alexander and Eckland, 1973).

Response rates. Although the problem of nonresponse is typically discussed as simply one component of the larger problem of completion rates (e.g., Daniel, 1975), it presents the researcher a unique set of problems which are different from those encountered in ensuring high sample coverage. In the most general sense this represents the problem of gaining compliance from the potential respondent. In the case of the personal interview, the introduction of the interview to the respondent is seen to be of critical importance (Cannell and Kahn, 1968: 578). Perhaps because of the personal nature of interviews (either face to face or telephone), their associated response rates are considerably higher than those obtained using mail-questionnaire methods. This may be due in part to the confounding of the issues of sample coverage and response rate which naturally occurs in mail surveys. In any case, the conventional wisdom indicates that despite the economy of mail questionnaires, their associated response rates are unacceptably low. A considerable amount has been written about the problems of nonresponse in the use of mail surveys. An excellent discussion of research in this area is Linsky's (1975) review of methods of increasing response rates for mail questionnaires.

One approach to obtaining greater cooperation in mail surveys which has gained recent attention in the literature is the personalization of the approach to the potential respondent (e.g., Andreasen, 1970; Hochstim and Athanasopoulos, 1970; Dillman, 1972). Prior research on personalization has produced mixed results (see Linsky, 1975).

Dillman and his associates (Dillman, 1972; Dillman and Frey, 1974; Dillman et al., 1974) have shown that through the use of a variety of personalization techniques simultaneously, response rates can be as high as 70% to 75% using mail questionnaires. A recent experiment by Carpenter (1974-1975) shows that response rates do favor the use of personalization methods, but he concludes that the reduction in rate of response in the least personalized conditions is not great.

There may be advantages to response rate resulting from the combination of different methods of data collection. Not only is it possible to improve sample coverage through the use of multiple methods of approach, potential respondents may react differently to different methods. The advantages for response rates of combining mail and other methods are well known. Of particular interest is the use of telephone interviews to supplement the mail questionnaire (Suchman and McCandless, 1940; Levine and Gordon, 1958; Donald, 1960; Eckland, 1965). Cost considerations may dictate the use of various combinations of mail, telephone, and personal interview methods to achieve the goal of high response rates (see Sudman, 1967, 1976a; Schmiedeskamp, 1962; Sharp, 1955; Kegeles et al., 1969).

The problem of gaining compliance from potential respondents poses unique problems in situations where formal consent procedures are used. The paper in this volume by Lueptow et al., "The Impact of Informed Consent Regulations on Response Rate and Response Bias," considers some of the problems associated with using protective consent procedures in surveys. Their study of high school seniors reveals that the use of parental-consent and self-consent methods does reduce rates of response, but does not substantially affect estimates of population parameters.

Item nonresponse. Respondents invariably do not answer all questions, and this may be a special problem where interviewers are absent. Several options are open to the researcher. He may omit all respondents with any missing information, treating the problem in the same manner as coverage and response problems generally. (See the discussion below on Weighting Data to Adjust Coverage and Response Bias.) Alternatively, it may be possible to make some optimal use of the data at hand, for example, by deleting cases for variables on a pairwise basis, or by supplying some estimate of the missing values. The approach of deleting all respondents with any missing data may drastically reduce the set of respondents with usable data, and any of these several approaches may introduce bias. The various approaches to handling missing data have been dealt with in the statistical literature (see e.g., the series of papers by Afifi and Elashoff, 1966, 1967, 1969a, 1969b), and these are discussed and evaluated in the paper, "Treating Missing Data in Multivariate Analysis," by Kim and Curry in the present volume. The Kim-Curry analysis suggests that pairwise deletion of missing data may have certain advantages over other methods in sociological data.

Weighting to adjust coverage and response bias. Procedures for weighting data in disproportionate stratified samples are well known and in common use (Smith, 1976). When description of the total population based on sample data is desired these methods are essential. It is often the case that certain sampling strata differ in the rate of coverage and/or response. This problem of disproportionate returns has been treated as equivalent to one of disproportionate sampling (U.S. Bureau of the Census, 1963; see also Fuller, 1974; Mandell, 1974; Filion, 1975-1976; Wayne, 1975-1976). Such weighting does not adjust for the *bias* due to noncoverage and/or nonresponse within sampling strata—it corrects only for differential representation rates among strata. In order to adjust for sample bias within strata, it is necessary to know the probability of an element's inclusion in the completed sample (see Fuller, 1974: 242). These are ordinarily not known, but several methods have been proposed to estimate these probabilities thereby providing a basis for adjusting the data. These are discussed and evaluated by Daniel (1975). The decision to weight data according to some assumed probability of response must be made with care. In any case, the consensus among survey methodologists seems to be that the use of methods to achieve high completion rates is of much greater importance than the use of methods to adjust data for potential bias (U.S. Bureau of the Census, 1963: 53).

RESPONSE ERRORS

It is well established that response variation on survey questions may result from a number of different errorful sources. Errors may be associated with (a) characteristics of the method; e.g., interviewer characteristics, question wording, question content; (b) characteristics of the respondent; e.g., memory, level of education, response sets; or (c) some interaction between respondent and method characteristics.

A *response error* for an individual is any discrepancy between the true value and the value observed in the survey. The behavior of these errors is of considerable concern to survey researchers, and as with sampling bias, steps are routinely taken to reduce such errors to a minimum. Illustrative of the survey researcher's concern with sources of error in survey methods is Sudman and Bradburn's (1974) review of over 900 papers and journal articles investigating sources of response error. The present section presents a summary of issues dealing with response errors under the headings: interviewer variability, question structure and sequence, methods of administration, and respondent errors.

Interviewer variability. It is often assumed that interviewers are a source of variation in responses to survey questions. Considerable research has been carried out relating interviewer characteristics to response errors (e.g., Feldman et al., 1951; Hyman, 1954; Hansen and Marks, 1958; Hochstim and Stock, 1951; Hansen et al., 1951; Williams, 1964, 1968, 1969; Weiss, 1968, 1969; Dohrenwend et al., 1968; Dohrenwend, 1969; Phillips and Clancy, 1972; Locander et al., 1976). A recent review of the literature on interviewer effects (Sudman and Bradburn, 1974: 109-117) indicates that with a few exceptions variation in responses from interviewers is trivial. The exceptions involve the interviewer characteristics of sex and race. There is some evidence that these characteristics matter when they are related to the topics covered by the survey (see Schuman and Converse, 1971; Hatchett and Schuman, 1975-1976). It is noteworthy, however, that Sudman and Bradburn end their review of the topic with the statement that "the quality of a survey depends on the interviewer's ability and not the interviewer's characteristics" (1974: 139). The paper in the present volume by Sudman et al., "Modest Expectations: The Effect of Interviewer Expectations on Response," refines the hypothesis regarding interviewer variability to focus on the effects of *interviewer expectations.* Using the best interviewers available to the National Opinion Research Center in a national probability sample, Sudman et al. find that as much as 5% to 10% of the variation in respondent reports of behavior lies between interviewers, but that most of this must be attributed to interviewer differences other than the interviewer's prior expectations.

Question structure and sequence. The presentation of questions in a survey, whether visually or aurally, may be more of an art than a science. This has not deterred researchers from attempting to assess the effects of question structure, e.g., closed versus open-ended, agree-disagree versus forced-choice alternatives, and the effects of the position of questions in the interview schedule. Sudman and Bradburn (1974: 33-34, 60) review the limited number of studies on question sequencing effects (see also Bradburn and Mason, 1964). Their review suggests that the effects of question order may be insignificant, but that more research on the problem is needed.

Although there is some history of a concern with the problem of question wording (e.g., McNemar, 1946) it has been ignored as a serious problem until recently (Schuman and Duncan, 1974; Presser and Schuman, 1975). Following Schuman and Duncan (1974: 249), the present discussion forces a distinction between error variation which occurs from the form of the question asked and the error which originates with the respondent, e.g., acquiesence response set (see discussion of "respondent errors" below). The paper by Schuman and Presser, "Question Wording as an Independent Variable in Survey Analysis," returns to the question-wording experiments of three decades ago in order to show that the effects of question wording on survey results are not trivial. It may be that question characteristics, e.g., agree-disagree versus forced choice, may combine with certain respondent characteristics, like acquiescence response set, to produce the resultant errors. The challenge to research in this area is to develop a model which specifies the question characteristics which combine with respondent characteristics to produce bias.

Method of administration. The dominant methods of administering a survey instrument are the self-administered questionnaire (usually, but not always, mailed to the sample), the personal interview and the telephone interview. It is often assumed that respondents will answer some types of questions differently in one form of administration compared to another. For example, it is sometimes suggested that personal interviews stimulate "socially desirable" or "socially acceptable" responses (e.g., Hyman, 1954: 139-145; Wiseman, 1972; Hochstim, 1967; Sudman, 1967: 54-57). One might conclude from this, as does Sudman (1967: 57), that the self-administered method would represent more accurate data. There is also some evidence which suggests that self-administered methods provide more accurate data when the survey material is threatening or involves a great deal of self-disclosure (see Sudman and Bradburn, 1974), but other evidence exists which casts doubt on the strength of such effects (e.g., DeLamater and MacCorquodale, 1975; Locander et al., 1976).

Sudman and Bradburn (1974) hypothesize that response errors are inversely related to the degree of task structure involved in the method of administering the questions, but are reluctant to order different methods along a unitary dimension of structure. They also hypothesize that the greater the problems of self-presentation for the respondent, the variability of response will be increased for behavioral reports, and decreased for attitude questions. Arranging the self-administered, telephone, and personal interview methods on a continuum of low to high self-presentation, their review of the available literature suggests support for the hypothesis regarding self-presentation. Further research is called for in comparing methods of administration in terms of response variability, response quality, and relative cost.

Respondent errors. Even when efforts are taken to reduce response errors which arise from question format, question content, interviewers, or method of administration, errors originating from the respondent are inevitable. Such errors may in fact be conditioned by such things as the method of administration, question threat, and so forth. In any case, when levels of respondent errors are unknown, as they almost always are, it becomes necessary to develop models of these errors so that their effects can be taken into account. Psychometricians and econometricians have contributed a great deal to the understanding of the consequences of error when it is random (e.g., Lord and Novick, 1968; Johnston, 1972). Classical test theory, in particular, provides several models for the behavior of random-measurement error which allows researchers to avoid its biasing effects given multiple measurements. Sociologists have also shown an interest in modeling respondent errors using causal models. The work of Siegel and Hodge (1968), Heise (1969), Costner (1969), Blalock (1968, 1969, 1970, 1971, 1974), Duncan (1972), Alwin (1973), among others is illustrative of the application of the algebra of path analysis to the modeling of respondent error using multiple indicators. More recently, the methods of the psychometrician and econometrician have been joined with the causal-modeling approaches to provide better solutions to these problems (e.g., Wiley and Wiley, 1970; Hauser and Goldberger, 1971; Alwin, 1974, 1976; Alwin and Tessler, 1974; Burt, 1973, 1976; Long, 1976; Wheaton et al., 1977; Hargens et al., 1976; Joreskog and Goldberger, 1975; Mason et al., 1976; Bielby et al., 1977a, 1977b; Joreskog and Sorbom, forthcoming; Joreskog, 1973). The work in this area shows that respondent error is not necessarily an illusive quantity. The paper in this issue by Bielby and Hauser, "Response Bias in Earnings Functions for Nonblack Males," illustrates the use of recently developed techniques for estimating structural equation models with unobserved variables. Their paper exemplifies the most sophisticated treatment of the problem of respondent errors by sociologists to date.

It would be a mistake to assume that all error in survey responses operates randomly. Indeed, survey researchers have studied a number of different sources of nonrandom error which are thought to originate within the respondent, for example, memory (Neter and Waksburg, 1964; U.S. Bureau of the Census, 1965; Gray, 1955; Sudman and Bradburn, 1973), acquiescence response set (Couch and Keniston, 1960; Campbell et al., 1967; Carr, 1971; Jackman, 1973; Phillips and Clancy, 1970), and social desirability (Edwards, 1957; Crowne and Marlowe, 1964; Dohrenwend, 1966; Phillips and Clancy, 1970, 1972). There are two sets of issues here. The first is to identify pertinent sources of nonrandom error. The literature cited here has done this to a considerable extent. The second is to develop some way of taking such error into account, and this has been done only to a limited extent. Social scientists have considered three types of solutions: (1) the specification of correlated error terms in measurement models (see e.g., Mason et al., 1976; Bielby et al., 1977a, 1977b); (2) the specification of general sources of method variance in measures having a common method (e.g., Joreskog, 1971; Alwin, 1974); or (3) the specification of specific sources of method variance in measures which result from individual sources (e.g., Jackman, 1973). These all have their advantages in certain circumstances, but we imagine that the direction for future research lies in the development of models which explicitly incorporate sources of nonrandom error, either as measured or unmeasured variables.

CLOSING

There are several issues related to the making of errors in surveys that we have not covered—issues of confidentiality and respondents' right to privacy (but see Lueptow et al. in this issue), issues of cost and efficiency in obtaining data via sample surveys, problems of using archival-survey data, the uses of modern computers and other technological advances in minimizing errors in data collection, transcription and storage, and others. For discussions of some of these issues the reader is encouraged to seek out other sources cited here which focus on these issues; e.g., Sudman (1976a).

We have tried to develop a framework for considering errors in surveys which incorporates strategies for dealing with errors both at the level of data collection and data analysis. While we believe it is impossible to remove all errors in the collection of data, or to remove potential error using data adjustments, we do believe that judicious attention to the problems of errors in surveys can increase the confidence we have in survey results.

The papers included in this issue (reviewed in the above discussion) investigate a number of issues covered by our general outline. We believe the papers are representative of the attention which sociologists are currently giving these problems. While many of these papers call into question the importance of certain sources of error, there appears to be a consensus among the authors that further research is needed in most of these areas. We look forward to the results which continued research into these questions will bring.

NOTE

1. This presentation may be confusing to those who ordinarily use the term "response rate" in place of the term "completion rate" as used here. Obviously, the particular terminology used is much less important than the distinction between the two classes of problems associated with obtaining "coverage" and "response."

REFERENCES

AFIFI, A. and R. M. ELASHOFF (1969a) "Missing observations in multivariate statistics III: Large sample analysis of simple linear regression." J. of the Amer. Statistical Association 64 (March): 337-358.
———(1969b) "Missing observations in multivariate statistics IV: A note on simple linear regression." J. of the Amer. Statistical Association 64 (March): 359-365.
———(1967) "Missing observations in multivariate statistics II: Point estimation in simple linear regression." J. of the American Statistical Association 62 (March): 10-29.
———(1966) "Missing observations in multivariate statistics I: Review of literature." J. of the Amer. Statistical Association 61 (September): 595-604.
ALEXANDER, K. L. and B. K. ECKLAND (1973) Effects of Education on the Social Mobility of High School Sophomores Fifteen Years Later (1955-1970). Institute for Research in Social Science. Chapel Hill: Univ. of North Carolina.

ALWIN, D. F. (1976) "Attitude scales as congeneric tests: A re-examination of an attitude-behavior model." Sociometry 39 (December): 377-383.

———(1974) "Approaches to the interpretation of relationships in the multitrait-multi-method matrix." Pp. 79-105 in H. L. Costner (ed.) Sociological Methodology 1973-74. San Francisco: Jossey-Bass.

———(1973) "Making inferences from attitude-behavior correlations." 36 (June): 253-278.

ALWIN, D. F. and E. L. JENSEN (1976) "A brief report on the combined use of mail and telephone methods of data collection." (May) [Unpublished].

ALWIN, D. F. and R. C. TESSLER (1974) "Causal models, unobserved variables and experimental data." Amer. J. of Sociology 80 (July): 58-86.

American Statistical Association (1974) "Report on the ASA conference on surveys of human populations." Amer. Statistician 28 (February): 30-34.

ANDREASEN, A. R. (1970) "Personalizing questionnaire correspondence." Public Opinion Q. 34 (Summer): 273-277.

BIELBY, W. R., R. M. HAUSER, and D. L. FEATHERMAN (1977a) "Response errors of nonblack males in models of the stratification process." J. of the Amer. Statistical Association 72 (Dec.).

———(1977b) "Response errors of nonblack males in models of the inter-generational transmission of socioeconomic states." Amer. J. of Sociology 82 (May) [forthcoming].

BLALOCK, H. M., Jr. (1974) Measurement in the Social Sciences: Theories and Strategies. Chicago: Aldine.

———(1971) Causal Models in the Social Sciences. Chicago: Aldine-Atherton.

———(1970) "Estimating measurement error using multiple indicators and several points in time." Amer. Soc. Rev. 35 (February): 101-111.

———(1969) "Multiple indicators and the causal approach to measurement error." Amer. J. of Sociology 75 (September): 264-272.

———(1968) "The measurement problem: a gap between the languages of theory and research," In H. M. Blalock and A. Blalock (eds.), Methodology in Social Research. New York: McGraw-Hill.

BRADBURN, N. M. and W. M. MASON (1964) "The effect of question order on responses." J. of Marketing Research 1 (November): 57-61

BRUNNER, J. A. and G. A. BRUNNER (1971) "Are voluntarily unlisted telephone subscribers really different?" J. of Marketing Research 8 (February): 121-124.

BURT, R. S. (1976) "Interpretational confounding of unobserved variables in structural equation models." Soc. Methods and Research 5 (August): 3-52.

———(1973) "Confirmatory factor-analytic structures and the theory construction process." Soc. Methods and Research 2 (November): 131-190.

Business Week (1973) "The public clams up on surveys taken." 15 (September): 216-220.

CAMPBELL, D. T., C. R. SEIGMAN and M. B. REES (1967) "Direction of wording effects in the relationships between scales." Psychological Bull. 68 (November): 292-303.

CANNELL, C. F. and R. L. KAHN (1968) "Interviewing," Ch. 15 in G. Lindzey and E. Aronson (eds.), The Handbook of Social Psychology. Reading, MA.: Addison Wesley.

CARPENTER, E. H. (1974-1975) "Personalizing mail surveys: a replication and re-assessment." Public Opinion Q. 38 (Winter): 614-620.

CARR, L. (1971) "The Srole items and acquiescence." Amer. Soc. Rev. 36 (April): 287-293.

CLARRIDGE, B. R., L. S. SHEEHY, and T. S. HAUSER (forthcoming) "Tracing members of a panel: a 17-year follow-up." In K. F. Schuessler (ed.), Sociological Methodology 1978. San Francisco: Jossey-Bass.

COOPER, S. L. (1968) "Random sampling by telephone: an improved method." J. of Marketing Research 1 (November): 45-48.

COSTNER, H. L. (1969) "Theory, deduction, and rules of correspondence." Amer. J. of Sociology 75 (September): 245-263.

COUCH, A. and K. KENISTON (1960) "Yeasayers and naysayers: agreeing response set as a personality variable." J. of Abnormal and Social Psychology 60 (March): 151-174.

CRIDER, D. M. and F. K. WILLITS (1973) "Respondent retrieval bias in a longitudinal survey." Sociology and Social Research 58 (October): 57-65.

CRIDER, D. M., F. K. WILLITS, and R. C. BEALER (1972) "Tracking respondents in longitudinal surveys." Public Opinion Q. 35 (Winter): 613-620.

DANIEL, W. W. (1975) "Nonresponse in sociological surveys: a review of some methods for handling the problem." Soc. Methods and Research 3 (February): 291-307.

DeLAMATER, J. and P. MacCORQUODALE (1975) "The effects of interview schedule variations on reported sexual behavior." Soc. Methods and Research 4 (November): 215-236.

DEMING, W. E. (1944) "On errors in surveys." Amer. Soc. Rev. 9 (August): 359-369.

DILLMAN, D. A. (1972) "Increasing mail questionnaire response in large samples of the general public." Public Opinion Q. 36 (Summer): 254-257.

DILLMAN, D. A. and J. H. FREY (1974) "Contribution of personalization to mail questionnaire response as an element of a previously tested method." J. of Applied Psychology 59 (June): 297-301.

DILLMAN, D. A., J. A. CHRISTENSON, E. H. CARPENTER, and R. BROOKS (1974) "Increasing mail questionnaire response: a four state comparison." Amer. Soc. Rev. 39 (October): 774-756.

DOHRENWEND, B. P. (1966) "Social status and psychological disorder: an issue of substance and an issue of method." Amer. Soc. Rev. 31 (February): 14-34.

DOHRENWEND, B. S. (1969) "Interviewer biasing effects: toward a reconcilation of findings. Comments by Barbara Snell Dohrenwend." Public Opinion Q. 33 (Spring): 121-125.

DOHRENWEND, B. S., J. COLOMBOTOS, and B. P. DOHRENWEND (1968) "Social distance and interviewer effects." Public Opinion Q. 32 (Fall): 410-422.

DONALD, M. N. (1960) "Implications of nonresponse for the interpretation of mail questionnaire data." Public Opinion Q. 24 (Spring): 99-114.

DUNCAN, O. D. (1972) "Unmeasured variables in linear models for panel analysis." Pp. 36-82 in H. L. Costner (ed.), Sociological Methodology, 1972. San Francisco: Jossey-Bass.

DUNKLEBERG, W. C. and G. S. DAY (1973) "Nonresponse bias and call-backs in sample surveys." J. of Marketing Research 10 (May): 160-168.

ECKLAND, B. K. (1965) "Effects of prodding to increase mail-back returns." J. of Applied Psychology 49 (June): 165-169.

———(1968) "Retrieving mobile cases in longitudinal surveys." Public Opinion Q. 32 (Spring): 51-64.

EDWARDS, A. (1957) The Social Desirability Variable in Personality Assessment and Research. New York: Dryden.

FELDMAN, J. J., H. H. HYMAN, and C. W. HART (1951-1952) "Interviewer effects on the quality of survey data." Public Opinion Q. 15 (Winter): 734-761.

FILION, F. L. (1975-1976) "Estimating bias due to nonresponse in mail surveys." Public Opinion Q. 39 (Winter): 482-492.

FRANCIS, J. D. and L. BUSCH (1975) "What we now know about 'I don't knows.' " Public Opinion Q. 39 (Summer): 219-226.

FRANKEL, L. R. (1976) "Statistics and people—the statistician's responsibilities." J. of the Amer. Statistical Association 71 (March): 9-16.

FULLER, C. H. (1974) "Weighting to adjust for survey nonresponse." Public Opinion Q. 38 (Summer): 239-246.

GLASSER, G. J. and G. D. METZGER (1975) "National estimates of nonlisted telephone households and their characteristics." J. of Marketing Research 12 (August): 359-361.

GROVES, R. M. (1977) "An empirical comparison of two telephone sample designs." Survey Research Center, Univ. of MI. (May) [Unpublished].

GRAY, P. G. (1955) "The memory factor in social surveys." J. of the Amer. Statistical Association 50 (June): 344-363.

HANSEN, R. H. and E. S. MARKS (1958) "Influence of the interviewer on the accuracy of survey results." J. of the Amer. Statistical Association 53 (September): 635-655.

HANSEN, M. H., W. N. HURWITZ, E. S. MARKS, and W. P. MAULDIN (1951) "Response errors in surveys." J. of the Amer. Statistical Association 46 (June): 147-190.

HARGENS, L. L., B. F. RESKIN, and P. D. ALLISON (1976) "Problems in estimating measurement error from panel data." Soc. Methods and Research 4 (May): 439-458.

HATCHETT, S. and H. SCHUMAN (1975-1976) "White respondents and race-of-interviewer effects." Public Opinion Q. 39 (Winter): 523-528.

HAUCK, M. and M. COX (1974) "Locating a sample by random digit dialing." Public Opinion Q. 38 (Summer): 253-260.

HAUSER, R. M. and A. S. GOLDBERGER (1971) "The treatment of unobservable variables in path analysis." Pp. 81-117 in H. L. Costner (ed.) Sociological Methodology 1971. San Francisco: Jossey-Bass.

HAWKINS, D. F. (1975) "Estimation of nonresponse bias." Soc. Methods and Research 3 (May): 461-488.

HEISE, D. R. (1969) "Separating reliability and stability in test-retest correlation." Amer. Soc. Rev. 34 (February): 93-101.

HOCHSTIM, J. R. (1967) "A critical comparison of three strategies of collecting data from households." J. of the Amer. Statistical Association 62 (September): 976-989.

———and D. A. ATHANASOPOULOS (1970) "Personal follow-up in a mail survey: its contribution and its cost." Public Opinion Q. 34: 69-81.

HOCHSTIM, J. R. and H. S. STOCK (1951) "A method of measuring interviewer variability." Public Opinion Q. 15 (Summer): 322-334.

HYMAN, H. (1954) Interviewing in Social Research. Chicago: Univ. of Chicago Press.

JACKMAN, M. R. (1973) "Education and prejudice or education and response-set? Amer. Soc. Rev. 38 (June): 327-339.

JOHNSTON, J. J. (1972) Econometric Methods. New York: McGraw-Hill.

JÖRESKOG, K. G. (1973) "A general method for estimating a linear structural equation system," pp. 85-112 in A. S. Goldberger and O. D. Duncan (eds.) Structural Equation Models in the Social Sciences. New York: Seminar Press.

————(1971) "Statistical analysis of sets of congeneric tests." Psychometrika 36 (June): 109-133.

JÖRESKOG, K. G. and D. SORBOM (forthcoming) "Statistical models and methods for analysis of longitudinal data," in D. J. Aigner and A. S. Goldberger, Latent Variables in Socioeconomic Models. Amsterdam: North-Holland Publishing.

KEGELES, S. S., C. F. FINK, and J. P. KIRSCHT (1969) "Interviewing a national sample by long-distance telephone." Public Opinion Q. 33 (Fall): 412-419.

KISH, L. (1965) Survey sampling. New York: John Wiley.

————(1949) "A procedure for objective respondent selection within the household." Amer. Statistical Association J. 44 (September): 380-387.

LUETHOLD, D. A. and R. J. SCHEELE (1971) "Patterns of bias in samples based on telephone directories." Public Opinion Q. 35 (Summer): 249-257.

LEVINE, S. and G. GORDON (1958) "Maximizing returns on mail questionnaires." Public Opinion Q. 22 (Winter): 568-575.

LINSKY, A. S. (1975) "Stimulating esponses to mailed questionnaires: a review." Public Opinion Q. 39 (Spring): 82-101.

LOCANDER, W., S. SUDMAN, and N. BRADBURN (1976) "An investigation of interview method, threat and response distortion." J. of the Amer. Statistical Association 71 (June): 269-275.

LONG, J. S. (1976) "Estimation and hypothesis testing in linear models containing measurement error: a review of Jöreskog's model for the analysis of covariance structures." Soc. Methods and Research 5 (November): 157-206.

LORD, F. M. and M. R. NOVICK (1968) Statistical Theories of Mental Test Scores. Reading, MA: Addison-Wesley.

MANDELL, L. (1974) "When to weight: determining nonresponse bias in survey data." Public Opinion Q. 38 (Summer): 247-252.

MASON, W. M., R. M. HAUSER, A. C. KERCKHOFF, S. S. POSS, and K. MANTON (1976) "Models of response error in student reports of parental socioeconomic characteristics," pp. 443-494 in W. H. Sewell, R. M. Hauser, and D. L. Featherman (eds.) Schooling and Achievement in American Society. New York: Academic Press.

McALLISTER, R. J., S. J. GOE, and E. W. BUTLER (1973a) "Tracking respondents in longitudinal surveys: some preliminary considerations." Public Opinion Q. 37 (Fall): 413-416.

McALLISTER, R. J., E. W. BUTLER, and S. J. GOE (1973b) "Evolution of a strategy for the retrieval of cases in longitudinal survey research." Sociology and Social Research 58 (October): 37-47.

McNEMAR, Q. (1946) "Opinion-attitude methodology." Psychological Bull. 43 (July): 289-374.

MORTIMER, J. T. and J. LORENCE (1977) "Locating respondents and inducing high response in a panel study." Univ. of Minnesota [Unpublished].

NETER, J. and J. WAKSBERG (1964) "A study of response errors in expenditures data from household interviews." J. of the Amer. Statistical Association 59 (March): 18-55.

PERRY, J., Jr. (1968) "A note on the use of telephone directories as a sample source." Public Opinion Q. 32 (Fall): 691-695.

PHILLIPS, D. L. and K. J. CLANCY (1972) "'Modeling effects' in survey research." Public Opinion Q. 36 (Summer): 246-253.

————(1972) "Some effects of 'social desirability' in survey studies." Amer. J. of Sociology 77 (March): 921-940.

————(1970) "Response bias in field studies of mental illness." Amer. Soc. Rev. 35 (June): 503-515.

RYDER, N. B. (1964) "Notes on the concept of a population." Amer. J. of Sociology 70 (March): 447-463.

SCHMIEDESKAMP, J. W. (1962) "Reinterviews by telephone." J. of Marketing 26 (January): 28-34.

SCHUMAN, H. and J. M. CONVERSE (1971) "The effects of black and white interviewers on white respondents in 1968." Public Opinion Q. 35 (Spring): 44-68.

SCHUMAN, H. and O. D. DUNCAN (1974) "Questions about attitude survey questions," pp. 232-251 in H. L. Costner (ed.) Sociological Methodology 1973-74. San Francisco: Jossey-Bass.

SCHUMAN, H. and S. PRESSER (1975) "Question wording as an independent variable in survey analysis: a first report." Preceedings of the Amer. Statistical Association, Social Science Section: 16-25.

SCHWIRIAN, K. P. and H. R. BLAINE (1966-1967) "Questionnaire-return bias in the study of blue-collar workers." Public Opinion Q. 30 (Winter): 656-663.

SEWELL, W. H. and R. M. HAUSER (1975) Education, Occupation, and Earnings: Achievement in the Early Career. New York: Academic Press.

SHARP, H. (1955) "The mail questionnaire as a supplement to the personal interview." Amer. Soc. Rev. 20 (December): 718.

SHARP, H. and A. FELDT (1959) "Some factors in a probability sample survey of a metropolitan community." Amer. Soc. Rev. 24 (October): 650-661.

SIEGEL, J. S. (1974) "Estimates of the coverage of the population by sex, race and age in the 1970 census." Demography 11: 1-23.

SIEGEL, P. M. and R. W. HODGE (1968) "A causal approach to the study of measurement error," pp. 28-59 in M. Blalock, Jr. and A. B. Blalock (eds.) Methodology in Social Research. New York: McGraw-Hill.

SMITH, K. W. (1976) "Analyzing disproportionately stratified samples with Computerized statistical packages." Soc. Methods and Research 5 (November): 207-230.

SUCHMAN, E. A. and B. McCANDLESS (1940) "Who answers questionnaires?" J. of Applied Psychology 24 (December): 758-769.

SUDMAN, S. (1976a) Applied Sampling, New York: Academic Press.

————(1976b) "Sample surveys," pp. 107-120 in A. Inkeles, J. S. Coleman, and N. Smelser (eds.) Annual Review of Sociology, Palo Alto, CA: Annual Reviews.

————(1973) "The uses of telephone directories for survey sampling." J. of Marketing Research 10 (May): 204-207.

————(1967) Reducing the costs of surveys. Chicago: Aldine.

————(1966) "New uses of telephone methods in survey research." J. of Marketing Research 3 (May): 163-167.

————and N. BRADBURN (1974) Response effects in surveys. Chicago: Aldine.

————and N. BRADBURN (1973) "Effects of time and memory factors on response in surveys." J. of the Amer. Statistical Association 68 (December): 805-815.

TAEUBER, C. and M. H. HANSEN (1964) "A preliminary evaluation of the 1960 Censuses of the Population and Housing." Demography 1: 1-13.

TROLDAHL, V. C. and R. E. CARTER, Jr. (1964) "Random selection of respondents within households in phone surveys." J. of Marketing Research 1 (May): 71-76.

U.S. Bureau of the Census (1976) Statistical Abstract of the U. S.: 1976. Washington, DC: GPO.
——— (1974a) Standards for Discussion and Presentation of Errors in Data. Technical Report No. 32. Washington, DC: GPO.
———(1974b) Indexes to Survey Methodology Literature. Technical Report No. 34. Washington, DC: GPO.
———(1965) Response Errors in Collection of Expenditures Data by Household Interviews: an Experimental Study. Technical Report No. 11. Washington, DC: GPO.
———(1963) The Current Population Survey, a Report on Methodology Technical Report No. 7. Washington, DC: GPO.
WAYNE, I. (1975-1976) "Nonresponse, sample size, and the allocation of resources." Public Opinion Q. 39 (Winter): 557-562.
WEISS, C. H. (1969) "Interviewer biasing effects: toward a reconciliation of findings, Comments by Carol H. Weiss." Public Opinion Q. 33 (Spring): 127-129.
———(1968-1969) "Validity of welfare mothers' interview responses." Public Opinion Q. 32 (Winter): 622-633.
WHEATON, B., B. MUTHEN, D. F. ALWIN, and G. F. SUMMERS (1976) "Specification and estimation of panel models incorporating reliability and stability parameters," in D. R. Heise (ed.) Sociological Methodology 1977. San Francisco: Jossey-Bass.
WILEY, D. E. and J. A. WILEY (1970) "The estimation of measurement error in panel data." Amer. Soc. Rev. 35 (February): 112-116.
WILLIAMS, J., Jr. (1969) "Interviewer biasing effects: toward a reconcilliation of findings, Comments by J. Allen Williams, Jr." Public Opinion Q. 33 (Spring): 125-127.
———(1968) "Interviewer role performance: a further note on bias in the information interview." Public Opinion Q. 32 (Summer): 287-294.
———(1964) "Interviewer role performance: a study of bias in the information interview." Sociometry 27 (September): 338-352.
WILLIAMS, W. H. (1970) "The systematic bias effects of incomplete responses." Public Opinion Q. 33 (Fall): 593-602.
WISEMAN, F. (1972) "Methodological bias in public opinion surveys." Public Opinion Q. 36 (Spring): 105-108.
WRIGHT, J. D. (1975) "Does acquiescence bias the 'index of political efficacy'?" Public Opinion Q. 39 (Summer): 219-226.

Duane F. Alwin is Associate Professor of Sociology at Indiana University. The present special issue of Sociological Methods and Research *grows out of his interest in the methods of survey research. More generally, his interests span the areas of quantitative methods, social psychology, education, and social inequality. At the moment, he is involved in research focusing on the familial and extra-familial sources of influence on the achievement plans and aspirations of adolescents.*

This paper renews the line of research into the effects of changes in survey question wording and form which occupied researchers during the 1940s. We suggest two reasons for the cessation of such research: the idiosyncratic nature of many of the items experimented with and the near exclusive focus on single-variable distribu- tions. In the present study, the experiments are based on decisions that face all survey investigators: whether to use agree-disagree statements or forced choice items; whether to ask open or closed questions; whether and how to balance al- ternatives offered; whether to include a middle alternative; and whether or not to filter for no opinion. Furthermore, we examine the consequences of these decisions not only for univariate distributions but also for an item's relationship to educa- tion. The results from SRC national probability samples suggest that for the first two types, as well as for items involving variations in tone of word, the decisions may affect inferences about correlations with education. For the other three types the effects are restricted mainly to changes in marginals, although the no-opinion type shows a more limited kind of interaction with education. Finally, we present evidence that index construction is not an adequate solution to the question- wording problem.

QUESTION WORDING AS AN INDEPENDENT
VARIABLE IN SURVEY ANALYSIS

HOWARD SCHUMAN
STANLEY PRESSER
The University of Michigan

*d*uring the 1940's a number of experiments on attitude question wording and form were carried out by both academic and com- mercial survey researchers seeking to determine whether different ways of asking the same attitude item led to different results. These experi-

AUTHORS' NOTE: *We are indebted to Jean M. Converse who worked with us in the development of the experiments described here, to Jane Fountain for statistical and computing advice, and to Otis Dudley Duncan and William M. Mason for advice on several important technical points. We alone are responsible for any errors. This research has been supported by grants from the National Institute of Mental Health (MH 24266) and the National Science Foundation (GS-39780 and Soc 76-15040). An earlier version of the paper was presented at the American Statistical Association meetings, Atlanta, August 1975.*

ments became most widely known through the Cantril et al. (1944) collection of papers on *Gauging Public Opinion* and Payne's little book, *The Art of Asking Questions* (1951). An example of such experiments is a pair of questions on freedom of speech reported by Rugg in 1941. One national sample was asked: "Do you think the United States should allow public speeches against democracy?" A comparable sample was asked: "Do you think the United States should forbid public speeches against democracy?" Approximately 20% more people were willing to "not allow" such speeches than were willing to "forbid" them—a difference suggesting that a seemingly innocuous word change can shift univariate item results noticeably.

By the early 1950s such question-wording experiments had largely disappeared from major surveys. We think there were several reasons for their demise. First, the basic fact that item marginals are in part a function of question wording was by then recognized, at least in theory, by virtually all academic survey researchers. Beyond repeatedly demonstrating the phenomenon, further experiments seemed to serve no particular purpose, as McNemar had observed in his extended review of "Opinion Attitude Methodology" in 1946. Of even greater importance, we believe, was the fact that almost all these early reports of experiments were restricted to univariate results, while survey *analysis* is typically concerned with relationships between variables. The assumption developed among investigators that marginals cannot be trusted owing to question wording uncertainties, but that associations between variables are not subject to this same sort of instability. Exactly this assumption is made, for example, by Stouffer and DeVinney in *The American Soldier* (1949: 168):

> one must be careful to focus attention on *differences* in percentages among different categories of men with favorable attitudes on a given item, not on absolute percentages. The fact that the percentages saying the Army was run pretty well or very well are large does not mean, necessarily, that so many men were actually favorable to the Army—such percentages are artifacts of question wording and of the check-list categories arbitrarily selected as 'favorable' .... But when we focus on *differences* in percentages responding favorably to the *same* questions, among men in different categories, the differences can be meaningful in a sense in which the absolute values cannot. [emphasis in original]

What Stouffer and DeVinney state explicitly appears, in the absence of warnings to the contrary, to have been assumed by many other survey methodologists and practitioners.[1]

The assumption of "form-resistant correlations," as we will call it, was further bolstered as academic survey analysts came to stress the use of attitude scales. On the one hand, this steered the analyst away from single-item percentage results, with their illusion of absolute proportions for and against specific social objects or positions. On the other hand, attitude scaling is intended to reduce idiosyncratic effects of individual items, though how this will necessarily eliminate *systematic* form effects is rarely spelled out.[2] It should be noted that use of scales or indices is often incomplete in even the best surveys; major variables may be constructed in this way, but parts of analysis frequently continue to draw on single-item variables because lack of time or anticipation prevents detailed measurement of every theoretical construct of interest.

Another reason for the decline of question wording experiments lay in the ad hoc character of most of the early work. Even in terms of univariate results, larger theoretical issues of question construction and typology were seldom addressed, and there was little concern to replicate findings or to estimate the frequency, magnitude, or underlying nature of question-wording effects. For this reason, wording experiments have come to be treated anecdotally, reported as illustrative warnings in most survey methods books, but not further developed theoretically or empirically.[3]

GOALS OF THE PRESENT RESEARCH

Our present research attempts to return to the question-wording experiments of three decades ago, but to do so with a different primary focus, a more systematic concern with types of survey questions (e.g., open versus closed), and some improvements in methodological procedure and analysis. The change in focus arose when Schuman and Duncan (1974), in the course of several different substantive analyses, came upon variations in question wording that seemed to affect bivariate as well as univariate distributions. These examples were at best suggestive, some being seriously defective from an experimental standpoint and others too ambiguous in terms of item wording to be representative of contemporary surveys. The present project was initiated as a more systematic attempt to test the hypothesis of form-resistant correlations, an attempt which grew to include development of a typology of question forms, as well as treatment of some related issues.

Two general hypotheses underlie this research. First, where question wording alters marginals appreciably, it seems unlikely from a theoretical standpoint that those persons being affected are simply a random subsample of all respondents. The effects are a kind of self-selection, and self-selection is rarely a randomizing procedure. Second, and more specifically, those affected by form should usually be the less educated, as well as the less interested or involved in the particular issues asked about. For the present paper, we concentrate on education because it is a fundamental variable in almost all survey analysis, and its interaction with question form would mean that one would draw different conclusions about the relation of education to opinion depending on which question form had been asked.

Our initial reasoning was that poorly educated respondents should be more easily swayed by emotionally toned words or by the presence or absence of a response alternative. Better educated respondents, on the other hand, should more easily grasp the general point of a question and not be as easily affected by emotionally colored words or by the degree to which implications of a response are spelled out. Furthermore, it seemed likely that more educated respondents would feel less deferential toward the interviewer and her questionnaire, and therefore more willing to insist on giving a sensible alternative answer (e.g., a midpoint between two extremes) even where it is not provided by the question frame. For these reasons, plus the general importance of years of schooling as both a cognitive and a status indicator, this seemed to us a strategic starting point for an analysis of question-form and wording effects.[4]

Types of Experiments and Results

We decided as part of our first set of experiments to replicate one of the question variations of earlier years, in part to gain some assurance that chance factors had not misled investigators about even univariate effects. For this purpose, we selected the forbid-allow example described earlier, using random divisions of the 1974 Survey Research Center Omnibus national sample.[5] The univariate results from 1940 and from 1974 are shown in Table 1. There is remarkably close replication in direction and degree of the wording effect after 34 years. The 21% difference in 1940 is paralleled by 16% in 1974, and thus the change over time is similar for both forms.[6] While we have no direct evidence as to the cause of the form effect, one possibility is that forbid is simply a more forbidding term than not allow, and that it is this difference in bluntness of language that makes some people less willing to deny freedom of speech when that form is used.

TABLE 1
Comparison of Forbid and Allow Marginals in 1940 and 1974

Allow Form			Forbid Form		
Do you think the United States should allow public speeches against democracy?			Do you think the United States should forbid public speeches against democracy?		
	1940	1974		1940	1974
1. Yes (Allow)	25%	56%	2. No (Not Forbid)	46%	72%
2. No (Not Allow)	75%	44%	1. Yes (Forbid)	54%	28%
	100%	100%		100%	100%
N	(*)	(494)	N	(*)	(936)

Response by Form, 1974 data only: $X^2_1 = 35.75$, p < .001

*N's for 1940 are not given in Rugg (1941) from which the earlier percentages are taken, but these were large national samples, presumably quota in design. Percentages for all distributions have been recomputed omitting DK responses; their inclusion does not change results appreciably.

Figure 1 shows the relation between response and education for the two question forms. In line with our hypothesis, form seems to make least difference (6%) for those who have been to college, but has a substantial impact (26%) on those with zero to eleven years of schooling; high school graduates fall in between. Using Goodman's (1971) method for analyzing multiway-contingency tables, the likelihood-ratio x^2 for the three-way interaction is 5.75, p < .06.[7] On replication in 1976, this three-way interaction reaches significance at beyond .02—the college-educated again showing the least effect—but the linear trend is not obtained, high-school graduates and those without high-school diplomas being affected about equally. Thus, tone of word makes a difference here not only in marginals but in a fundamental bivariate relationship. In both forms, to be sure, there is a positive relation of education to civil-libertarian sentiment; however, the relation is not only stronger for one form, but, by having both forms, our understanding of the difference in crystallization of these sentiments by education is enhanced. Moreover, it is conceivable that a larger gap in connotation or tone of word would remove entirely the association with education on one form, thus changing conclusions about type as well as degree of relationship to this basic background variable.

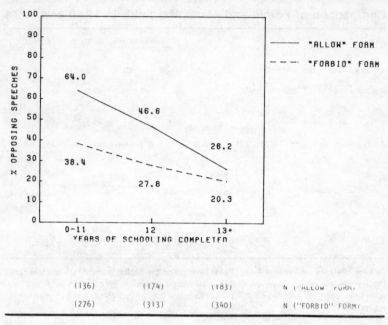

Figure 1: Percent Opposing Free Speech by Education and Form, 1974

These findings point to the danger of survey analysis with single-item opinion variables, even where one is interested entirely in associations, not in marginals. Furthermore, while one might assume that index construction would remove just this type of idiosyncratic effect, we shall also raise some questions about that strategy in a later section of this paper. For now, we must admit that apart from its cautionary message, the forbid-allow example is not a very constructive one, since it would be difficult to predict in advance the effects of other variations in verbal connotation, and impossible to generalize from it to other types of items.

With this latter problem in mind, we constructed most of our other experiments to test *types* of question form, rather than using purely idiosyncratic examples. Taking the point of view of the survey investigator faced with the need to create or select a pool of attitude items, we noted certain decisions that typically need to be made—and that usually are made on the basis of rule-of-thumb, personal preference, convenience, or simply chance. This led us to formulate five question types, though they are clearly not completely exclusive of one another in either conception or operation. We shall briefly describe and illustrate each of the five types. Note that in constructing examples of each question type, we started, wherever possible, from items used in past national surveys, in order to increase the external validity of our results.

(1) *Agree-Disagree versus Forced Choice.* Speed and convenience of administration frequently seem to recommend the use of agree-disagree items in questionnaires and interviews. But some past research, as well as a certain intuitive regard for fairness in presentation of issues, suggests the desirability of providing forced-choice forms, rather than single propositions to be accepted or rejected. We have thus far tested this type of form variation in five experiments. Two use items dealing with the causes of crime and with the political role of women, respectively, and the other three employ questions concerning foreign policy issues. All five show form differences in marginals significant beyond the .05 level, and two of the five provide significant three-way interactions with education, as illustrated in Table 2.

The item on crime presented in Table 2 involves three forms: two separate agree-disagree statements that are logical contraries (A & B) and a forced choice version (C). Responses to both the first agree-disagree form and the forced choice form show a significant relationship to education, but those on the other agree-disagree form show no such relationship. Thus one would draw different conclusions about the *existence* of a relationship to education in this case, not only about its magnitude. The response by education by form interaction reaches significance in the comparison of the two agree-disagree forms, and is of borderline significance in the B-C comparison. Moreover, in the latter case, the three-way interaction with education occurs despite almost identical marginals! One would not have had even the initial clue of a two-way difference (response by form) to alert one to the possibility of this important interaction.

Although in only one of the other experiments (women in politics) does the three-way interaction with education reach significance, in three of the remaining four the variation in response by form is greatest for the least educated just as it is in the crime example. Thus, overall, the assumption of form-resistant correlations is not well supported with respect to these agree-disagree items.

TABLE 2
Agree-Disagree Example
Percent Saying Individuals Are to Blame for Crime
by Education and Form*

		Total	Education		
			0-11	12	13+
A. Please tell me whether you agree or disagree with this statement: "Individuals are more to blame than social conditions for crime and lawlessness in this country." (Do you agree or disagree?)	% Agreeing N	59.6 (473)	67.7 (133)	62.0 (163)	51.7 (176)
			$x_2^2 = 8.55$ p < .02		
B. Please tell me whether you agree or disagree with this statement: "Social conditions are more to blame than individuals for crime and lawlessness in this country." (Do you agree or disagree?)	% Disagreeing N	43.2 (472)	41.9 (136)	41.8 (153)	45.3 (181)
			$x_2^2 = 0.54$ n.s.		
C. Which in your opinion is more to blame for crime and lawlessness in this country--individuals or social conditions?	% Individuals N	46.4 (448)	55.3 (141)	44.5 (155)	40.5 (148)
			$x_2^2 = 6.76$ p < .05		

	A&B	A&C	B&C
Response by Form: $x_1^2 =$	25.55	16.12	0.96
	p < .001	p < .001	n.s.
Response by Education by Form: $x_2^2 =$	6.64	0.67	4.98
	p < .05	n.s.	p < .10

*Form C is a slight modification of a Gallup question. See "The Gallup Opinion Index," Report No. 65, November 1970, page 15.

(2) *Formal versus Substantive Balance.* A second and related type of issue that has concerned attitude survey investigators is that of balancing interrogative items. For example, the first question in Table 3 asks about gun control in the briefest way possible, following a form that

TABLE 3
Balancing Example
Percent Favoring Gun Control by Education and Form*

	Total	Education		
		0-11	12	13+
A. Would you favor a law which would require a person to obtain a police permit before he could buy a gun?	71.0	68.9	70.8	72.7
	(455)	(119)	(168)	(165)
		$x_2^2 = 0.49$, n.s.		
B. Would you favor <u>or</u> oppose a law which would require a person to obtain a police permit before he could buy a gun?	71.7	69.9	71.6	72.6
	(455)	(103)	(162)	(179)
		$x_2^2 = 0.24$, n.s.		
C. Would you favor a law which would require a person to obtain a police permit before he could buy a gun, <u>or</u> do you think such a law would interfere too much with the right of citizens to own guns?	67.3	62.5	63.9	73.4
	(431)	(96)	(166)	(169)
		$x_2^2 = 4.80$, p < .10		

Response by Form (A and B): $x_1^2 = 0.05$, n.s.

Response by Form (B and C): $x_1^2 = 2.00$, n.s.

None of the response by education by form interactions is significant.

*Forms A and B were taken with slight modification from Gallup questions. See pages 2027 and 2077 of Volume 3 of *The Gallup Poll*, New York: Random House, 1972.

was often used in surveys in earlier years. Probably in response to criticism that this type of format discouraged negative answers, the second form, in one wording or another, has tended to replace it.[8] We call this an example of "formal balancing," and our hypothesis was that it would have little or no effect, since the original form is a question rather than an assertion and negative answers are clearly implied as legitimate. An example of what we call "substantive balancing" is shown in the third version, where another side of the issue is not only stated, but justified. We hypothesized that this type of an opposing argument would lead to changes in response distribution.

We tested four different items using both kinds of balance—that is, with three form variations for each test. As predicted, the addition of a formal alternative produces virtually no change in univariate percentages. (In one case, there is a significant difference in 1974 but upon replicating that experiment in 1977 we obtained no difference at all, hence the original finding is probably best regarded as a chance event.) Not surprisingly, in all four cases the substantive variation produces the larger difference from the unbalanced form—reliably different from it in three of the four experiments, the nonsignificant exception being the gun control item. (In a replication of the gun control experiment the substantive effect did reach significance. See Schuman and Presser, 1977, for a detailed examination of those results.) However, in *none* of the four experiments does the variation, either formal or substantive, significantly affect the response by education relationship. Unlike the agree-disagree versus forced-choice problem, we cannot reject the null hypothesis for three-way form effects, at least in relation to education.

(3) *Middle Alternatives*. When forced-choice questions *are* employed, frequently there is a logical middle alternative, as in the example on Vietnam aid shown in Table 4. Investigators sometimes choose to omit the middle alternative in order to produce an easier-to-work-with dichotomous question, on the assumption that most respondents opting for the middle position do in fact lean one way or the other. For the four items that we varied in this way, all show significant differences in the middle-category percentage, but in no case does the division of opinion between the polar positions differ significantly by form. This is particularly striking because in one instance the middle alternative rises by almost 40% and yet the ratio between the other positions is unaffected.

Turning to the results by education, the form-resistant correlation assumption fares quite well for this type of item. In no case does the response by education by form interaction approach significance. This is so whether one collapses the polar positions and compares them with the middle alternative or simply compares the polar positions, excluding the middle alternative.

(4) *Opinion Screening Filters*. It is well known that on many issues a large fraction of the public has no opinion, for reasons of lack of information or interest. In asking survey questions, one can attempt first to screen out those who admit having no opinion, as the Institute for

TABLE 4
Middle Alternative Example
Aid to Vietnam by Education and Form*

Looking back, do you think our government did too much to help the South Vietnamese government in the war, or not enough to help the South Vietnamese government?

	Total	Education		
		0-11	12	13+
Too Much	71.7%	65.2%	73.5%	75.2%
(If Volunteered) Right Amount	17.2	22.0	17.3	13.4
Not Enough	11.1	12.8	9.2	11.3
	100 (882)	100 (250)	100 (294)	100 (335)

$$X_4^2 = 9.95, p < .05$$

Looking back, do you think our government did too much to help the South Vietnamese government in the war, not enough to help the South Vietnamese government, or was it about the right amount?

	Total	Education		
		0-11	12	13+
Too Much	62.0%	57.6%	55.4%	72.0%
Right Amount	28.8	34.5	34.5	18.2
Not Enough	9.2	7.9	10.1	9.8
	100 (434)	100 (139)	100 (148)	100 (143)

$$X_4^2 = 13.65, p < .01$$

Response by form (collapsing "too much" and "not enough"): $X_1^2 = 22.62, p < .001$
Response by form (excluding "right amount"): $X_1^2 = 0.04$, n.s.
None of the response by education by form interactions is significant.

*Modeled after the Vietnam items analyzed in Schuman and Duncan (1974).

Social Research election studies have done for many years. This step has the seeming merit of reducing the number of what Converse (1970) has called nonattitudes. However, the effect of such screening on substantive distributions appears not to have been carefully studied, and there is some uncertainty whether and how to compare items with and without such filters.

TABLE 5
No Opinion Filter Example
Russian Intentions by Education and Form*

Here are some questions about other countries. Not everyone has opinions on these questions. If you do <u>not</u> have an opinion, just say so. "The Russian leaders are basically trying to get along with America." Do you have an opinion on that? (IF YES) Do you agree or disagree?

| | Total | Education | | |
		0-11	12	13+
No Opinion	37.6%	58.5%	37.1%	21.9%
Agree	39.2	25.9	34.9	53.5
Disagree	23.1	15.6	28.0	24.6
	100 (510)	100 (147)	100 (175)	100 (187)

$$x_4^2 = 52.05, p < .001$$

Here are some questions about other countries. Do you agree or disagree with this statement? "The Russian leaders are basically trying to get along with America."

| | Total | Education | | |
		0-11	12	13+
(IF VOLUNTEERED) No Opinion	15.2%	27.2%	12.7%	7.9%
Agree	49.9	39.7	47.1	60.5
Disagree	34.9	33.1	40.1	31.6
	100 (499)	100 (151)	100 (157)	100 (190)

$$x_4^2 = 29.81, p < .001$$

Response by form (collapsing "agree" and "disagree"): $x_1^2 = 66.72$, p <.001
Rssponse by form (excluding DK): $x_1^2 = 1.24$, n.s.
None of the response by education by form interactions is significant.

*Constructed for this experiment.

To study this problem we constructed three items dealing with foreign affairs, intentionally varying the presumed familiarity of the issue for respondents. One item dealt with the Soviet Union, one with the Middle East, and one with the 1974 revolution in Portugal which had occurred just prior to the survey. We took this to represent an ascending order of public ignorance. The two forms that comprised this set of experiments are illustrated in Table 5 by the pair of questions about the Soviet leaders.

Several conclusions can be drawn from these three experiments. First, it clearly is possible to increase substantially the percentage of "don't know" (DK) responses by making their legitimacy clear—the increase being 22% in the Soviet example and about the same in the others. Second, while the univariate change in DK's as such is highly reliable in each case, when all DK responses are removed there is no significant univariate difference between the two forms. In other words, the ratio of the agree to disagree responses is very similar across form in each experiment, despite the shift of approximately a quarter of the respondents between DK and substantive categories. Third, omitting DK responses, substantive distributions do not differ in their relation to education between the two forms. That is, the response (agree versus disagree) by education by form interaction does not approach significance for any of the three foreign policy items.

It is also of some interest to collapse the substantive responses into a single category ("opinion") as against the DK or no opinion category. When this is done, the three-way interaction (education by form by opinion versus DK) is not significant for any of the three items, but for two of the items (the Middle East and Portugal) the linear component of the interaction reaches borderline levels (p = .10).[9] Moreover, if each item is dichotomized into DK versus all nonDK responses, and the three recoded items are summed to form a "DK index," then the correlation of DK with education is -.39 on the filtered version and -.26 on the unfiltered. (The difference between the two correlations is significant beyond the .05 level, and the same significance level is obtained for the corresponding regression coefficients.) Thus, education is more highly correlated (negatively) with saying DK when the latter is explicitly offered than when it is merely accepted if volunteered. This suggests that in cases where education is very strongly related to opinion position (which is not so in the present examples), filtering, by changing the educational distribution of those who give an opinion, would alter the marginal split between the substantive positions.

One incidental finding from these three graded items is the percentage of people willing to say DK to difficult questions even when not explicitly encouraged. It is sometimes asserted that people are willing to answer *any* survey question, but this is not the case at least on these foreign policy issues. On the form which does not screen out DK responses, 15% of the sample nevertheless volunteered DK to the Soviet item, 23% to the Middle East item, and fully 63% to the item on Portugal. We did not expect many people to have an opinion about the Portuguese revolution in the fall of 1974, and more than three-fifths of the sample were willing to admit this even on the form that did not encourage such admission.

(5) *Open versus Closed Questions.* The oldest controversy over question form involves the issue of open versus closed questions. On the one hand, the open form does not limit respondents to alternatives within the investigator's frame of reference, and it also avoids suggesting or imposing answers the respondent may not have considered. On the other hand, the closed form restricts responses to those germane to the researcher's aims, and provides data in a form that is a great deal easier to code and analyze. The issue at hand, however, is whether and when the two forms yield basically the same results. Given the antiquity of the controversy (see Lazarsfeld, 1944, for an early but still widely read statement), the general absence of split-ballot comparisons of the two forms is remarkable.

We designed three open-closed experiments, but have analyzed only one thus far for presentation here. The experiment actually involved two stages. First, the standard closed form of a question on work values (see Lenski, 1963, and the NORC General Social Surveys) was asked of a random half of the 1976 Detroit Area Study (DAS), and a comparable open version was asked of the other half. This produced a number of sizeable differences between the forms, but these were difficult to interpret because it is possible they were due simply to defects in the specific closed alternatives employed. The latter may never have been properly developed to correspond to open responses (as Lazarsfeld, 1944, recommended), or they may simply have become out of date since the closed question was first devised in the late 1950s. In order to remedy this, we reconstructed the closed question to provide categories and wording more in keeping with the actual responses obtained in the 1976 DAS open form. This new version of the closed question, shown in Table 6, was then used with a parallel open form in a split-ballot experiment in a 1977 SRC national telephone survey.[10]

Although there are a number of significant differences in the results obtained on the two forms in 1977, for reasons of space we focus here only on one of the more interesting ones. As may be seen in Table 6, almost three times as many people (21%) choose the answer "work that is steady with little chance of being laid off" on the closed version as give a comparable answer on the open form (8%). Apparently a fair number of people think of this as an important job attribute when reminded of it, yet do not think of it unaided. Moreover, the form difference is related to education. The poorly educated are most likely to choose the job security category on the closed version, but least likely to choose it on the open. We are unable to tell which form (if either) provides the more valid picture of the relation between education and concern with security, but clearly one would draw different conclusions depending on the form used. Since for other alternatives in this experiment the two forms lead to similar conclusions (e.g., the higher educated are more likely to emphasize "feeling of accomplishment" as most important on both forms), open-closed differences are by no means inevitable and an analyst should probably feel most comfortable when the same result can be obtained regardless of form.

Further analysis and presentation of this and other open-closed experiments is deferred until a later report. For now, it is apparent that for at least some important comparisons, the assumption of form-resistant correlations must be rejected when open and closed versions of the same basic item are under consideration.

INDEX CONSTRUCTION

We would like to address one more issue in this paper: whether index construction, at least in a typical form in which it occurs, necessarily minimizes the interactive problems that constitute our primary concern here. In addition to the five main types of items described thus far, two more miscellaneous items were taken from Stouffer's well-known study, *Communism, Conformity, and Civil Liberties* (1955). Although Stouffer was a master craftsman in the construction of survey questions, we noticed that the items shown on the left side of Table 7 were worded in a way that might discourage civil-libertarian responses, much as the "not allow" form in the example with which we opened this paper. We therefore wrote slightly different versions of the two items which leaned, we think not unfairly, in the more libertarian direction (see Table 7, right side). The two original Stouffer items were placed in the same form as the item on "allowing" speeches against democracy; the two amended items in the form with the "forbid" speeches item. By scoring each item as 1 or 2, and adding these scores, we created a brief

TABLE 6
Open-Closed Example
Percent Saying Security is Most Important by
Education and Form*

	Total	Education		
		0-11	12	13+
This next question is on the subject of work. People look for different things in a job. Which one of the following five things would you most prefer in a job? Work that pays well; Or work that gives a feeling of accomplishment; Or work where there is not too much supervision and you make most decisions yourself; Or work that is pleasant and where the other people are nice to work with; Or work that is steady with little chance of being laid off.	21.0 (590)	32.0 (128)	21.0 (210)	14.8 (244)

$$x^2_2 = 14.67 \quad p < .001$$

	Total	Education		
This next question is on the subject of work. People look for different things in a job. What would you most prefer in a job?	7.7 (469)	3.6 (84)	13.2 (152)	5.6 (233)

$$x^2_2 = 9.44 \quad p < .01$$

Response by Form: $x^2_1 = 29.57 \quad p < .001$

Response by Education by Form: $x^2_2 = 10.98 \quad p < .01$

*Percents represent those who chose the category "work that is steady with little chance of being laid off" on the closed version and those who gave a comparable answer on the open version.

"civil liberties index" for each form.[11] Let us call the first form the "hard form," the second the "easy form," in terms of encouraging a libertarian position. The correlation of this index with education is .34 for the easy or facilitative form, .51 for the hard. Although the two correlations are in the same direction, they differ significantly ($p < .01$), and education can be said to account for more than twice the variance in index scores for the hard form than for the easy one. (The difference between the two regression coefficients is also significant beyond the .01 level).[12] Thus it appears that the general problem we address in this paper is not one that can always be finessed by mechanical resort to index construction. This

TABLE 7
Two Civil Liberties Items Based on Stouffer (1955)

Original Stouffer Items	Our Variations
This next question is about a man who admits he is a Communist. Suppose he wrote a book which is in your public library. Somebody in your community suggests the book should be removed from the library. Would you favor removing the book, or not?	This next question is about a man who admits he is a Communist. Suppose he wrote a book which is in your public library. Somebody in your community suggests the book should be removed from the library. Somebody else in your community says this is a free country and it should be allowed to remain. Would you favor removing the book, or not?
There are always some people whose ideas are considered bad or dangerous by other people. For instance, somebody who is against all churches and religion. If such a person wanted to make a speech in your (city/town/community) against churches and religion, should he be allowed to speak, or not?	There are some people who are against all churches and religion. If such a person wanted to make a speech in your (city/town/community) against churches and religion, should he be allowed the freedom to speak, or not?

is not necessarily to argue against index construction—on the contrary, our work with individual items makes it clear that they are sometimes very unstable—but simply to note that many of the simple additive indices used in social research may be subject to cumulative biases of the kind dealt with in this study.

SUMMARY

Overall, it appears fairly easy to change item marginals to a reliable extent, although we should add that most substantive changes in marginals were under 15% and the average was closer to 5%. For agree-type items, open as against closed items, and for some items involving changes in tone of word, three-way interactions with education occur such that one would draw different conclusions from different forms of what can reasonably be thought of as the same basic question. Thus for these types of question, the assumption of form-resistant correlations appears to be a poor one. The assumption may be more justified, however, with two other types of items discussed: formal versus substantive balance and middle alternatives. We are unable to show that inferences about the relationship of education to opinion differ reliably by form in these cases. Finally, the no-opinion filter type occupies a middle ground. Education interacts with form to affect the don't know responses, but for the items used in our experiments, once DKs are excluded from analysis, form does not affect the relationship between education and substantive opinion.

Even where education is unrelated to form effects, this does not mean that such effects are random in nature. For example, in the no-opinion area we have discovered that the relations among attitudes on our experimental items differs by form. In the middle alternative area, there is evidence that intensity is related to form effect, people who say they feel strongly about their opinion showing much less difference between forms than those who register weaker intensity. Thus, while additional experiments are needed to understand the extent, causes, and differential validity of results obtained when the same question is asked in two or more ways, our work suggests that form effects occur with enough frequency so that researchers need to be wary of correlations based entirely on a single question form.

NOTES

1. More recent statements of the assumption may be found in Davis (1971: 20; and 1976: 37). Most textbooks we have looked at simply have nothing to say on the issue one way or the other.

2. An important exception is the work done during the 1940s by Guttman and Suchman (in Stouffer et al., 1950). However, their solution requires a very strong scaling model which is frequently not satisfied. For a brief critique of their work see Presser (1977: ch. 1).

3. One further reason for the cessation of work in this area may have had to do with the interests of the commercial pollers who provided the funds for many of the early investigations. It is hard to see how the continued display of question effects could be to the advantage of firms that encourage reliance on single-item distributions.

4. There is also some research showing education to be a significant interactive variable with respect to one question-form effect, agreeing-response set (see, for example, Lenski and Leggett, 1960; and Jackman, 1973). (This area is the one exception to our earlier statement that research into form effects ceased in the early 1950s.) At the same time, it should be recognized that years of schooling might promote interaction of an opposite sort, where subtle logical features of a question are noted only by the best educated (see Schuman and Harding, 1964).

5. Randomization was done systematically at the housing unit level. (Irene Hess, head of the SRC Sampling Section, constructed the subsampling design.) Since in some experiments we wished to compare three forms of a question, we created three equal-sized subsamples of about 500 each. Where only two forms were used, as in the forbid-allow experiment, one was allocated to two of the subsamples, the third to the remaining one.

6. Table 1 may be seen as presenting a three-way interaction involving question wording, response, and time. Lacking the 1940 frequencies, we cannot test the interaction for significance, but because the differences by form are so similar in the two years, the main finding appears to be constancy of form effect over time.

7. Significance levels reported in this paper must be regarded as approximations since we have used SRS tests, even though the SRC national samples involve some clustering. We computed more exact sampling errors (taking into account the clustering) for all the bivariate results reported and in no case did this change an inference.

8. This evolution in wording is particularly apparent in Gallup questions, as shown in another of our project papers: Converse, "A Content Analysis of National Survey Questions Across Organizations and Over Time" (unpublished, SRC, 1975).

9. For all these analyses we assume a logistic response model, as employed in the Goodman procedures. It may be noted that the Russia item shown in Table 5 reveals large variations in the DK percentage differences by form among the three educational groups: 31.3%, 24.4%, and 14.0% for the 0-11, 12, and 13 + groups, respectively. If a linear probability model is assumed, the response (opinion versus DK) by education by form interaction turns out to be significant ($\chi^2 = 7.92$, p $<$ .02 as computed by H. M. Kritzer's program, NONMET). Thus computations based on the two different models yield quite different conclusions, presumably because of floor effects on DK responses for the standard form. In accord with what seems to be dominant statistical thinking, we have based our main conclusions on results with the Goodman procedure and thus the logistic model, though it might be argued that floor effects have meaningful substantive implications in these no opinion experiments.

10. There were actually five versions of the closed item varying randomly the order of the response alternatives. Since the distributions are not significantly affected by this factor, we have collapsed over the five.

11. The average interitem correlation on each form was about .45.

12. The same results were obtained when we replicated the three experiments in 1976: the difference between the two correlations (.38 and .50) is significant at the .02 level.

REFERENCES

CANTRIL, H. et al. (1944) Gauging Public Opinion. Princeton: Princeton Univ. Press.

CONVERSE, P. E. (1970) "Attitudes and non-attitudes; continuation of a dialogue," pp. 168-189 in E. R. Tufte (ed.) The Quantitative Analysis of Social Problems. Reading MA: Addison-Wesley.

DAVIS, J. A. (1971) Elementary Survey Analysis. Englewood Cliffs, NJ: Prentice Hall.

——— (1976) "Are surveys any good, and if so, for what?" pp. 32-38 in H. W. Sinaiko and L.A. Broedling (eds.), Perspectives On Attitude Assessment: Surveys and Their Alternatives. Champaign, Il: Pendleton.

GOODMAN, L. (1971) "The analysis of multidimensional contingency tables: stepwise procedures and direct estimation methods for building models for multiple classification," Technometrics 12: 33-61.

JACKMAN, M. R. (1973) "Education and prejudice or education and response-set?" American Soc. Rev. 38: 327-339.

LAZARSFELD, P. F. (1944) "The controversy over detailed interviews: an offer for negotiations." Public Opinion Q. 8: 38-60.

LENSKI, G. (1963) The Religious Factor. Garden City, NY: Anchor.

———and J. C. LEGGETT (1960) "Caste, class and deference in the research interview." Amer. J. of Sociology 65: 463-467.

McNEMAR, Q. (1946) "Opinion-attitude methodology!" Psych. Bul. 43: 289-374.

PAYNE, S. L. (1951) The Art of Asking Questions. Princeton: Princeton Univ. Press.

PRESSER, S. (1977) "Survey Question Wording and Attitudes in the General Public." Ph.D. dissertation, University of Michigan (unpublished).

RUGG, D. (1941) "Experiments in wording questions: II." Public Opinion Q. 5: 91-92.

SCHUMAN, H. and O. D. DUNCAN (1974) "Questions about attitude survey questions," pp. 232-251 in H. L. Costner (ed.) Sociological Methodology 1973-1974. San Francisco: Jossey-Bass.

SCHUMAN, H. and J. HARDING (1964) "Prejudice and the norm of rationality." Sociometry 27: 353-371.

SCHUMAN, H. and S. PRESSER (1977) "Public opinion and legislative inaction on gun registration." Public Opinion Q. (forthcoming).

STOUFFER, S. A. (1955) Communism, Conformity, and Civil Liberties. Garden City, NY: Doubleday.

STOUFFER, S. A., et al. (1950) Measurement and Prediction. Princeton: Princeton Univ. Press.

STOUFFER, S. A., et al. (1949) The American Soldier: Adjustment During Army Life. Princeton: Princeton Univ. Press.

Howard Schuman is Professor of Sociology and Program Director in the Survey Research Center, University of Michigan. He is presently Editor of Sociometry and has previously served as Director of the Detroit Area Study at Michigan.

Stanley Presser is a Research Investigator in the Survey Research Center, University of Michigan.

This paper measures the effect of interviewers and interviewers' prior expectations on response to threatening questions. The results indicate that interviewers are responsible for an average of about 7% of total response variance, to which expectations contribute a small amount. In most practical situations, interviewer expectations can be ignored.

MODEST EXPECTATIONS

The Effects of Interviewers'
Prior Expectations on Responses

SEYMOUR SUDMAN
University of Illinois at Urbana-Champaign

NORMAN M. BRADBURN
University of Chicago

ED BLAIR
University of Houston

CAROL STOCKING
University of Chicago

a possible source of response effects in survey measurement is the interviewer's expectations about respondents' answers. Interviewers' expectations might cause response effects in several ways. The interviewer may communicate her expectations to the respondents, who may try to fulfill these expectations. The interviewer may lead respondents with probes, or may fail to probe unclear or inappropriate answers, and record what the respondent meant to say. Also, the interviewer may incorrectly record answers without asking the questions. The extent of expectation effects is not well understood. This paper reports some analyses of interviewers' expectations and response variation.

Expectations about a study may be formed before or after entering the field. Prior expectations may relate to means and distributions of results. Hyman et al. (1954) describe "probability expectations," in which the interviewer anticipates a certain distribution of responses

---

AUTHOR'S NOTE: *This research was supported by National Science Foundation Grant GS-43203.*

and presumably tries to fulfill that distribution. Rosenthal and his associates (see, for example, Rosenthal, 1966) have studied hypothesis fulfillment in psychological experiments where prior expectations about differences in the mean scores of subject groups somehow are fulfilled.

Prior expectations may also relate to anticipated difficulty in asking the questions of the survey, to respondent uneasiness about answering the questions, or to data quality variables such as levels of overreporting or underreporting and percentages of "no answer" responses. Presumably, interviewers who anticipate difficulty with a study or high item nonresponse will be less aggressive about pursuing vague, evasive, or improbable responses or will communicate a lack of self-confidence to the respondent.

Question-sensitivity and data-quality expectations can also arise situationally within the interview. Hyman et al. (1954) distinguish two types of situational expectation—"role expectation" and "attitude structure expectation." Role expectation arises from identification of the respondent with some social role. For example, the interviewer might typecast a well dressed respondent with a large house as a business executive and form concomitant expectations about that respondent's attitudes, behaviors, and socioeconomic characteristics. Attitude structure expectation results from expectation of cognitive consistency; early responses generate expectations about responses for later items.

One would expect situational expectation effects to be more powerful than prior expectation effects. However, prior expectation effects would be easier to detect. Situational effects would be distinguishable only with very careful monitoring of expectations and answers or with confederate respondents who varied their responses according to prior instruction. Prior expectation effects would show up in between-interviewer variation.

Almost no research on prior expectations has ever been reported in the survey-methods literature, and almost no new results on situational expectations have been reported in the last 20 years. Sudman and Bradburn (1974) provide a reason for this neglect in their review of research into response effects. They contend that interviewer related variables, including interviewers' expectations, are much less powerful than task variables such as question threat in causing response effects. This implies that interviewer related variables should not receive high priority in investigations of response effects.

Empirical results of studies into expectation effects do not contradict Sudman and Bradburn's claim. The most spectacular demonstrations of expectation effects almost surely contain inflated effects. Rosenthal's experimenter expectation findings are laboratory based, and are subject to the amplification of effects which often occurs in the laboratory as compared with the field. Smith and Hyman's (1950) demonstration of attitude structure expectation effects used confederate respondents who presented extreme points of view with extreme consistency before giving a vague response. More naturalistic studies which measure interviewer variation without considering expectation, such as Hanson and Marks (1958), show 5% or less of total response variance as being attributable to interviewer variation.

However, this does not mean that expectation effects should be ignored. Interviewers do seem to contribute some small amount of variance to survey results, and studies of expectation do show effects, even if inflated. This paper contains data from a study which estimated interviewer effects in addition to some larger sources of response effects. One important variable in the study was respondents' perceptions of social norms against discussing topics. In an effort to see how much of this social uneasiness was interviewer related, we obtained interviewer expectations of general-study difficulty, specific-question difficulty, and respondent uneasiness. We also obtained expectations of overreporting or underreporting levels and of no-answer rates. This information allowed us to separate prior expectation effects from total interviewer related variance.

METHOD

The results are from a national U.S. sample survey of 1,172 respondents conducted by the National Opinion Research Center in 1975. In each of 50 primary sampling areas which fell into the sample, the best interviewer available was used (two or three interviewers were used in some areas). These interviewers were all female, mostly age 35-50, and generally had substantial previous experience. The study contained threatening questions placed within the framework of a leisure-activity study. After opening with questions about general recreational activities such as going to a movie, dining at a restaurant for pleasure, going bowling, playing golf, listening to the radio, and watching television, the study asked a series of questions on satisfaction and happiness. These items were followed with the threatening questions concerning gambling, drinking and getting drunk, smoking marijuana, using stimulant or depressant drugs, and sexual behavior.

Interviewer expectations were measured by a self-administered questionnaire which each interviewer completed after the training for this study, but before any interviewing had been conducted. The questionnaire asked the following questions:

In general, how easy or difficult to ask do you expect this survey to be?

How difficult to ask do you expect each section to be?

How uneasy do you expect each section to make most respondents?

Which groups of people, if any, do you expect to feel at least moderately uneasy about answering the questions in each section?

About what proportion of respondents do you expect will not answer each section?

Do you expect the total results from each section to report less behavior than actually is done by the respondents, about the correct amount of behavior or more behavior than actually is done?

It was hypothesized that response effects on threatening questions would be influenced by question form, respondents' perceptions of social norms against discussing the topic, and interviewer effects. The effects of question form and social uneasiness are discussed in other papers (Blair et al., 1977; Bradburn et al., 1977). Relative to these effects, interviewer effects were expected to be small. However, these effects were expected to be statistically significant and of practical importance except for very threatening questions such as masturbation, where an overpowering social norm would swamp interviewer effects, or very uncommon behaviors such as stimulant and depressant usage, where data would be too thin to show stable effects. The analysis of interviewer variation confirmed this expectation. No interaction effects between interviewers and question forms were expected, nor were any observed.

INTERVIEWER CONTRIBUTION
TO TOTAL VARIANCE

Tables 1A and 1B present the first stage of analysis, the estimates of interviewer contribution to total variance. The major problem

TABLE 1A
Percentage of Total Variance Due to
Interviewer, Using SS /SS as a Measure

Item	Interview Location				
	Non–Southern SMSA	Non–Southern Non–SMSA	Southern SMSA	Southern Non–SMSA	Weighted Average
N interviewers/N respondents	(37/634)	(7/164)	(10/212)	(5/126)	
Gambling Scale	14	5	8	8	11
Income	11	4	4	4	8
Ever smoke marijuana	10	5	8	4	8
Intercourse past month	9	3	10	1	8
Petting or kissing past month	9	3	7	2	7
Ever drink liquor	9	6	5	2	7
Ever drink wine	7	9	6	5	7
Ever drink beer	6	9	5	5	6
Ever use "uppers"	6	1	6	6	6
Ever use "downers"	7	5	3	1	6
social activities	6	6	2	7	6
Leisure activities	7	1	4	4	5
Masturbation past month	6	3	6	2	5
How often intoxicated past year	6	7	4	2	5
AVERAGE	8	5	6	4	7

in interpreting these results is that interviewers were not randomly assigned to cases. Each interviewer worked within her home area, and typically only one interviewer worked an area. The total sample of interviewers consisted of 59 interviewers in 50 areas. Thus, it is not possible to separate area and interviewer effects. In Tables 1A and 1B, the most obvious location variables are controlled by presenting figures separately for non-Southern Standard Metropolitan Statistical Areas (SMSAs), non-Southern non-SMSAs, Southern SMSAs, and Southern non-SMSAs.

Table 1A shows that interviewers generally account for about 7% of the total response variance when the proportion explained is measured by the ratio of the sum of squares between interviewers to the total sum of squares. These figures have been controlled for respondent's education. Two other variables of interest, respondent's age and respondent's tendency to give socially desirable answers (as measured by an abbreviation of the scale developed by Crowne and Marlowe, 1960), were not controlled because they did not vary across interviewers.

The proportion of variance explained by interviewers is generally stable across items and locations. Non-Southern SMSAs have slightly higher proportions which probably are due to a more heterogeneous group of interviewers and a slightly smaller average case load. The F-ratios associated with the figures in Table 1A show interviewer effects as large or larger than those described by Hanson and Marks (1958) for demographic items.

Table 1B is presented because of a methodological weakness of the between-interviewer sum of squares to total sum of squares measure. That measure is simple to compute and has an intuitive meaning, but it is affected by changing the case load per interviewer. If the total sum of squares is roughly constant for a fixed number of respondents, one would increase the between-interviewer sum of squares, and thus the proportion of variance explained by increasing the number of interviewers, or reducing the case load. This problem can be corrected by using an analysis of variance analog to R^2 called $\hat{\omega}^2$, which adjusts for the number of treatment levels. The formula for $\hat{\omega}^2$ is:

$$\hat{\omega}^2 = \frac{SS_B - (k-1) MS_{res}}{SS_T + MS_{res}}$$

where SS_B is the between-group (interviewer) sum of squares, k is the number of interviewers, MS_{res} is the mean square of the residual, and SS_T is the total sum of squares.

Of course, using $\hat{\omega}^2$ as a measure reduces the amount of variance attributable to interviewers. Table 1B shows figures which range around 2%. While these percentages are small relative to question form effects and actual differences in individual behavior, they are about as large as the combined effects of the two location variables.

Both of the measures used to form Tables 1A and 1B are legitimate indicators of the proportion of variance explained by interviewers. The ratio of between to total sums of squares is a more understandable measure; however, one must remember that it will change somewhat with a case load different from the 20 case average used in this study. Both measures show small but generally significant interviewer effects on response variation. These interviewer effects may be caused by interviewer appearance, behavior, situational expectations, prior expectations, or some combination of these factors. Only a small proportion is attributable to prior expectations.

TABLE 1B
Percentage of Total Variance Due to Interviewers, Using ^{2} as a Measure

Item	Interview Location				
	Non-Southern SMSA	Non-Southern Non-SMSA	Southern SMSA	Southern Non-SMSA	Weighted Average
N interviewers/N respondents	(37/634)	(7/164)	(10/212)	(5/126)	
Gambling scale	9	1	3	4	6
Income	6	0	0	1	4
Ever smoke marijuana	5	1	3	0	4
Intercourse past month	4	0	5	0	3
Petting and kissing past month	4	0	3	0	3
Ever drink liquor	3	2	0	0	2
Ever drink wine	2	6	2	1	2
Ever drink beer	0	5	1	1	1
Ever use "uppers"	1	0	1	3	1
Ever use "downers"	2	1	0	0	1
Social activities	1	2	0	3	1
Leisure activities	2	0	0	1	1
Marturbation past month	0	0	1	0	0
How often intoxicated past year	0	2	0	0	0
AVERAGE	3	1	1	1	2

EXPECTATIONS ABOUT GENERAL STUDY DIFFICULTY

Interviewers' expectations about the general difficulty of the interview appear to be weakly related to levels of reporting. Table 2 indicates that interviewers who anticipated difficulties with the questionnaire obtained lower percentages of respondents who reported ever engaging in activities than interviewers who thought the survey would be very easy.

For the gambling, drinking, and sex items, interviewers who expected the interview to be very easy obtained levels of reporting 12% to 4% higher than interviewers who expected the interview to be difficult. These results seem unambiguous, but are statistically significant only for beer drinking.

For some of the variables the data do not show a linear trend. That is, while there is a difference between interviewers who think the interview will be very easy and those who think it will be difficult, the results in the middle bounce around. The small number of interviewers in each group accounts for the way the data bounce across columns. Combining interviewers who expected the study to be easy

TABLE 2
Response Related to Interviewer Expectations of General Difficulty

Item	Very easy	Easy	Neither easy nor difficult	Difficult	Ratio of very easy to difficult	R^2
Ever drink beer	86	84	76	73	1.18	.11
Ever drink liquor	90	83	82	78	1.15	.04
Ever drink wine	88	84	79	78	1.12	.02
Gambling scale	1.17	1.08	1.03	.98	1.19	.02
Intoxicated in past year	36	29	33	28	1.29	.01
Petting and kissing past month	81	75	80	71	1.14	.01
Intercourse past month	74	67	70	66	1.12	.01
Leisure Activities	4.46	4.43	4.50	4.19	1.06	0
Social Activities	41.31	35.86	34.41	34.89	1.18	0
Ever smoked marijuana	21	20	21	22	.95	0
Income	$12,216	$13,531	$14,041	$11,747	1.04	0
N respondents	(136)	(343)	(342)	(256)		
N interviewers	(7)	(18)	(18)	(13)		

NOTE: Numbers are percentage of respondents reporting this behavior, except for gambling scale, leisure, social activities, and income where means are presented.

with those who expected it to be very easy would somewhat stabilize the data, and would reduce the large differences on the sex items. The proportions of variance explained by interviewers' expectations of general difficulty range from 11% for beer down to 1 or 2% for most other items. While these results do show some effect of prior expectations, other interviewer variables and what goes on in the interview are clearly far more important.

Cooperation rate proved unrelated to general difficulty expectations of interviewers. Measures such as total doors approached, total refusals, and refusals from men and women did vary substantially by interviewer, but were unrelated to interviewer expectations.

EXPECTATIONS ABOUT LEVEL OF REPORTING

Interviewers who expected their respondents to underreport behavior obtained lower levels of reporting, thus confirming the notion of the self-fulfilling prophecy. Table 3 shows that the interviewers

TABLE 3
Response Related to Interviewer Expectations
of Respondent Reporting Level

Item	Expect correct or overreporting	Expect Underreporting	Ratio	R^2
Income	$13,750 (764/39)	$11,622 (247/17)	1.18	.06
Intercourse past month	69 (746/40)	67 (287/16)	1.03	.04
Intoxicated in past year	30 (462/23)	32 (644/33)	.94	.02
Gambling scale	1.08 (846/43)	.93 (262/13)	1.16	.01
Petting and kissing past month	78 (789/41)	71 (296/15)	1.10	.01
Ever drink beer	80 (742/37)	76 (374/19)	1.05	.01
Ever drink wine	82 (742/37)	78 (374/19)	1.05	0
Ever drink liquor	83 (742/37)	79 (374/19)	1.05	0

NOTE: Number of respondents above slash, number of interviewers below.

who expected respondents to underreport obtained lower reporting on 8 of 13 items and higher reporting on 3. The differences are smaller than those in Table 2 except for the item on income. A difference of $2,000 separates the average incomes reported to interviewers who expected income to be reported correctly or overreported and interviewers who expected income to be understated. The proportions of interviewer variance explained by interviewer expectations of over- or underreporting range from 6% for income down to 1% or less.

Expectations about level of reporting and expectations about the general difficulty of the interview are correlated, but not highly. Correlations between the items measuring anticipated level of reporting and the item measuring general expected difficulty all have absolute values less than .26. These fairly small correlations would lead one to expect even sharper response effects when both expectations are combined. Table 4 shows this to be the general case, with the proportions of explained variance slightly higher for most items.

Table 4 is formed by splitting the data into six groups. Expectations of whether the general interview will be easy, neither easy nor difficult, or difficult are cross-classified with expectations of whether or not the respondent will underreport. This table is a reminder of the small sample size that results when interviewers and not respondents are the independent observations. The final column is blank for the intercourse items, because no interviewers who expected the interview to be difficult also expected underreporting on these items. Splitting

TABLE 4
Response Related to Interviewer Expectations of General Difficulty and Level of Respondent Reporting

Item	Easy Correct under or over		Neither Correct under or over		Difficult Correct under or over		Ratio of first to last column	R^2
Ever drink beer	85	83	75	78	80	66	1.29	.11
Income $	$13,663	11,290	14,649	12,652	12,424	10,767	1.27	.06
Ever drink liquor	86	83	82	81	83	73	1.18	.04
Intercourse past month	70	67	72	68	66	--	----	.04
Ever drink wine	86	83	77	82	84	71	1.21	.02
Gamblin scale	1.15	.90	1.07	.90	1.03	.83	1.39	.02
Intoxicated in past year	27	33	32	34	35	23	1.17	.01
Petting and kissing past month	80	66	82	76	69	78	1.03	.01

56 interviewers six ways causes substantial sampling variability, and these results must be treated as suggestive rather than conclusive.

OTHER EXPECTATIONS

Interviewer expectations also were measured for expected difficulty with each section of the interview, expected respondent uneasiness, specific groups of people expected to feel uneasy about sections of the interview, and anticipated proportion of respondents who would not answer various sections. These expectations had no additional impact upon the data.

Previous analyses have shown that respondent uneasiness has powerful effects upon levels of reporting (Bradburn et al., 1977). However, interviewer expectations of respondent uneasiness have no effects. Correlations between interviewers' expectations and respondents' actual uneasiness are near zero. Interviewer expectations about uneasiness appear to say something about the interviewer, not about the respondent.

Expectations about proportion of respondents who will not answer are unrelated to actual no-answer rates because variation between interviewers is just too small for effects to appear. No-answer responses are less than 1% of total responses for all items except intercourse, masturbation, and income, and are under 5% for those items.

CONCLUSION

The introduction of this paper suggested that interviewers' prior expectations can affect survey data. For the behaviors reported in this paper, it is evident that these expectations have, at most, very small effects. In most practical situations these effects are trivial and could be ignored.

Nevertheless, these findings suggest two ideas for minimizing interviewer effects. First, interviewers who expect a study to be difficult should not be hired for that study. This study used the best interviewers available to NORC and further screened them with a practice interview. Despite this procedure, general difficulty expectations had some level effects. Second, interviewers should not be trained to expect underreporting. The behaviors measured in this study are under-reported (Blair et al., 1977). However, telling this to the interviewers would aggravate the problem.

A previous paper has suggested data adjustment based on respondent uneasiness (Bradburn et al., 1977). Data adjustment is not an appropriate way to deal with interviewer expectation effects because of the small sample sizes of interviewers and the resulting high sampling variances.

Small sample sizes keep the data in this paper from being conclusive. This problem is inherent in research about interviewer expectations: few studies are likely to employ hundreds of interviewers. Replication will be the only way to establish precisely the nature and magnitude of interviewer-expectation effects.

REFERENCES

BLAIR, E., S. SUDMAN, N. M. BRADBURN, and C. STOCKING (1977) "How to ask questions about drinking and sex: response effects in measuring consumer behavior." J. of Marketing Research, 14: 316-321.

BRADBURN, N. M., S. SUDMAN, E. BLAIR, and C. STOCKING (1977) "Question threat and response bias." (working paper).

CROWNE, D. P. and D. MARLOWE (1960) "A new scale of social desirability independent of psychopathology." J. of Consulting Psychology 24: 349-354.

HANSON, R. and E. MARKS (1958) "Influence of the interviewer on the accuracy of survey results." J. of the Amer. Statistical Association 53: 635-655.

HAYS, W. (1963) Statistics for Psychologists. New York: Holt, Rinehart & Winston.

HYMAN, H. et al. (1954) Interviewing in Survey Research. Chicago: Univ. of Chicago Press.

ROSENTHAL, R. (1966) Experimenter Effects in Behavior Research. New York: Appleton-Century-Crofts: Sect. 2.

SMITH, H. and H. HYMAN (1950) "The biasing effect of interviewer expectations on survey results." Public Opinion Q. 14: 491-506.

SUDMAN, S. and N. M. BRADBURN (1974) Response Effects in Surveys. Chicago: Aldine.

Seymour Sudman is Professor of Business Administration, Sociology, and the Survey Research Laboratory, University of Illinois at Urbana-Champaign.

Norman M. Bradburn is chairman, Department of Behavioral Sciences and Senior Study Director at the National Opinion Research Center, University of Chicago.

Ed Blair is Assistant Professor of Marketing at the University of Houston.

Carol Stocking is an Associate Study Director, National Opinion Research Center, University of Chicago.

This paper reports an analysis of nonparticipation and bias in a survey research project conducted among seniors in 18 high schools under the federal "informed consent" regulations. Three major findings emerge. First, the use of voluntary participation and (among students under 18) parental consent procedures reduced the participation rate sharply from that obtained in a similar survey in 1964. However, the reduced participation did not introduce much bias into three criterion measures for which population data were available: mean intelligence score, mean GPA, and the intelligence-GPA correlation. Third, we found that bias in these measures on a school-by-school basis was not strongly correlated with the participation rate, suggesting that researchers need to consider factors other than the response rate in assessing the amount of bias in survey research on high school populations.

THE IMPACT OF INFORMED CONSENT REGULATIONS
ON RESPONSE RATE AND RESPONSE BIAS

LLOYD LUEPTOW
SAMUEL A. MUELLER
University of Akron
RICHARD R. HAMMES
University of Wisconsin-Oshkosh
LAWRENCE S. MASTER
Keystone Area Education Agency,
Dubuque, Iowa

*t*his paper reports some of the research consequences of carrying out a large-scale survey among high school seniors under the new federal regulations pertaining to privacy and informed consent. These regulations have arisen from instances of harm to subjects in

AUTHORS' NOTE: *This project was supported by funds from the Office of the Assistant Secretary for Planning and Evaluation, Department of Health, Education and Welfare, and benefited from comments and suggestions to an earlier report received from the Project Officer Keith Baker. This report does not necessarily reflect the position of HEW on any conclusion or interpretation. The survey administration was carried out under an award from the Faculty Research* medical research (see Katz, 1972), but similar concerns have arisen from the use of human subjects in laboratory experiments in psychology (Baumrind, 1971; Kelman, 1972; Sykes, 1967). With some exceptions (i.e., American Sociological Association's Code of Ethics, 1968; Dorn and Long, 1974; Galliher, 1973), sociologists have paid little attention to these issues, probably because sociological research normally involves substantially less risk to subjects than either medical research or some types of psychological research.

Published discussion focuses on three types of risks to research subjects: harm, deception, and loss of privacy. Harm appears to be most likely in social-psychological experiments where the subject is placed under considerable emotional stress (i.e., Milgram, 1963; for commentary and debate see Baumrind, 1964; Milgram, 1964; Steiner, 1972; and Gergen, 1973). Sociological research rarely involves this type of potential harm. Deception, however, is common in social-psychological experiments in sociology as in psychology. Although deception introduces issues of ethics rather than of harm, there has also been a long-standing concern with this dimension (Vinacke, 1954; Kelman, 1965; Baumrind, 1971).

Violation of privacy is of most concern to sociological researchers because of the pervasiveness of survey research, participant observation, and the use of records and archives, all of which raise issues of confidentiality. While we found no published evidence of any significant disclosure of confidential information by sociologists engaged in such research, the public is currently most sensitive to this dimension because of the continuing revelations of invasion of privacy in Watergate and post-Watergate investigations. This public concern became law in the Buckley Amendment to the Family and Educational Privacy Act of 1974, which treats the unauthorized use of questionnaire and archival data about students as invasion of privacy (Davis, 1975). This liability raises numerous questions for administrators (Chase, 1975; Cutler, 1975), and, as Davis (1975) notes, it is likely to increase the difficulty of conducting research requiring the use of student records.

Committee, University of Akron. We are grateful for the support and cooperation of the following Wisconsin high schools: Appleton East, Appleton West, Berlin, Bonduel, Brillion, De Pere, Fond du Lac Goodrich, Green Bay Preble, Kimberly, New London, Omro, Oshkosh North, Oshkosh West, Reedsville, Ripon, Southern Door, Wild Rose, Winneconne and Wittenburg—Birnamwood. We benefited from discussion with McKee McClendon and from editorial comment on a number of central points in this final analysis and presentation.

These various concerns about protecting the rights of subjects have been met by procedures established by the Department of Health, Education, and Welfare in 1974 and amended in 1975 (45 C.F.R. part 46). The central protective concept of the new procedures is that of "informed consent." Persons of majority status (including students eighteen and over in most jurisdictions) must indicate, through a signed statement, that they have been informed of the possible risks involved in the research and have consented to participate. A parent's signature on such a form is necessary for students under 18. The danger for research projects is that these operations may produce a sample of consenting respondents that may not be representative of the entire population.

Rosenthal and Rosnow (1975) have shown that volunteer subjects do tend to be different along a number of personality and social dimensions, both in the general population and in populations of college students. However, studies of bias associated with volunteering in high school are relatively rare, and no study has yet estimated the amount of bias introduced by parental nonconsent as distinct from self consent. For that matter, no study has yet estimated the bias introduced by self-consent under these new, formal consent procedures in any population. This paper is intended to provide new evidence in these respects, as well as to replicate and extend the evidence on bias in volunteer samples reviewed by Rosenthal and Rosnow (1975).

THE DATA

The data on which this paper is based were gathered in the spring of 1975 in 18 public high schools in a midwestern state. These data replicate data collected in these schools in 1964 and will be used in a study of change in occupational and educational dimensions of sex roles.[1]

In order to meet the requirements of privacy and informed consent that applied to this research, a consent procedure was developed that utilized a detachable (and identifying) face sheet on the questionnaire. Students were assembled and then given the questionnaire with its detachable face sheet. The face sheet described the study as a replication of the 1964 survey and described the study goals as (1) obtaining information about the high school and (2) obtaining information about the changes in educational and occupational orientations of the students themselves. It then indicated that student records would be used in the research and that participation was voluntary and had no connection with formal school requirements. The student was asked to fill out his name and address and sign the consent statement if he were an adult, or to detach the face sheet and take it home for his parent's signature if he were a minor. Each student also entered a random nine digit code number on both the consent form and the questionnaire. All students who were willing to participate were asked to fill out the questionnaire, which they did almost without exception. Consequently, in taking the consent forms home for signature, minor students left behind a completed, but totally unidentifiable instrument that could not be used in this research unless matched to a returned, signed, parental consent form. The signed consent forms were retained by the school counselors for use in collating student record information with the questionnaire information.

SPECIFIC PROBLEM

The data will permit examination of several consequences of these informed consent procedures and of the characteristics of bias in this type of research. First, we will examine the loss of cases from the use of voluntary informed consent and compare the relative loss of cases under parental consent with the loss under student consent procedures. As sex, intelligence, and grade point have been shown to be important factors in consent (Rosenthal and Rosnow, 1975; Wicker, 1968), we will examine those factors also, considering the net effect each has upon response rate—a control not common in the research reviewed by Rosenthal and Rosnow (1975). (We do not have data on socioeconomic status [SES] and other variables that might be of interest.) We will also observe the effects of school size and type of survey administration upon response rate, although these later two variables are confounded in a manner precluding clear resolution of independent effects in this study.

Second, we will examine bias in grade point and measured intelligence and in the correlation between them. Grades and intelligence are appropriate variables for this purpose, as they index a wide range of social and educational circumstances. The correlation between them represents the application of student ability to the academic purposes of the school, and consequently provides an index of the orientation of the student toward the academic programs (see Coleman, 1961: 263-264, for a classic application of this principle). In addition, accumulating research findings (Sewell and Hauser, 1975; and Alexander and Eckland, 1975, for illustrations and citations) have shown that intelligence also serves to mediate the effect of SES on grades and to independently affect teacher and parent encouragement for the son to attend college. Rosenthal and Rosnow (1975) have shown bias in intelligence and in grades, but to our knowledge, no one has yet examined the bias in the correlation between these variables. (Sewell and Hauser [1975] report little difference in the intelligence-grade point correlations of sons of responding and nonresponding parents.)

Finally, the data will permit us to examine the relationship between response rate and amount of bias. By treating each school as a separate population, we can shed some light on a much-discussed but little-investigated question in survey research: What constitutes a good or bad response rate on a survey? Although almost every methodology text contains some sort of discussion of this question, there is almost no empirical evidence on this issue. In an attempt to provide some rules of thumb, notwithstanding, Babbie (1973: 165) describes a response rate of 50% as "adequate for analysis," one of 60% as "good," and one of 70% as "very good." Sewell and Hauser (1975: 41) state that their (unreported) analysis indicates accurate estimates of sample values require a response rate of 80% or more. The present data can be used to provide new evidence and a rough evaluation of these guide-lines.

FINDINGS

Response Rates.

It is clear from the distributions in Table 1 that the use of volunteer participants resulted in a substantial loss of cases. In 1964, virtually 100% of the students in these schools had participated in the research when the participation was presented as a school requirement. Under the climate of the early 1960s, the survey administration was carried out in the high schools as an accepted and unquestioned school activity. In 1975, on the other hand, regulations on privacy and protection

TABLE 1
Study Participation by Type of Consent, Grade Point, Sex, and Intelligence.

		Male				Female				Total			
		Parental Consent		Student Consent		Parental Consent		Student Consent		Parental Consent		Student Consent	
Intell	GPA	% Part	Tot. Cases	% Part	Tot. Cases	% Part	Tot. Cases	% Part	Tot. Cases	% Part	Tot. Cases	% Part	Tot. Cases
low	low	32.0	(122)	63.2	(367)	37.0	(108)	68.2	(255)	34.3	(230)	65.3	(622)
	med	35.7	(28)	65.2	(112)	47.2	(72)	72.7	(143)	44.0	(100)	69.4	(255)
	high	40.0	(10)	63.6	(22)	36.4	(33)	68.3	(63)	37.2	(43)	67.1	(85)
med	low	33.7	(98)	63.2	(193)	35.8	(67)	55.6	(99)	34.5	(165)	60.6	(292)
	med	40.8	(71)	66.0	(153)	45.0	(100)	63.9	(147)	43.3	(171)	65.0	(300)
	high	49.0	(51)	81.0	(100)	53.7	(149)	73.6	(178)	52.5	(200)	76.3	(278)
high	low	20.0	(45)	70.3	(74)	38.5	(13)	71.4	(21)	24.1	(58)	70.5	(95)
	med	38.3	(81)	72.5	(131)	55.6	(45)	67.2	(61)	44.4	(126)	70.8	(192)
	high	47.7	(172)	82.6	(235)	52.2	(247)	79.9	(289)	50.4	(419)	81.1	(524)
	Total	37.4	(729)	68.9	(1509)	46.4	(883)	70.5	(1349)	42.4	(1612)	69.7	(2858)

of human subjects required voluntary participation. In addition, school administrations under the new and somewhat ambiguous regulations (Cutler, 1975) were less inclined to coerce students to participate. It is also likely that the 1975 students were less conforming and less intimidated by the formal authority of school administrators and research staff who administered the survey in each high school.

Thus in 1975, even though the survey was sponsored and scheduled by each high school administration, only 59.8% of the 4470 graduating seniors in these 18 high schools were included in the research. While various unobserved changes in the school circumstances between 1964 and 1975 were certainly involved in these differences, it seems likely that a large portion of the reduction in participation from 1964 to 1975 was due to the factor of voluntary participation. However, we have no way of knowing exactly what actually was the unique effect of the voluntary procedure.

We are in a better position to assess the response effect of parental consent as compared to student consent procedures. Table 1 shows that compared to student consent, parental consent procedures are very costly to the collection of data in this type of research. While 69.7% of the adult students, who could give their own consent, participated in the study, only 42.4% of the minors who required parental consent were included.[2]

Expected sex differences in response rate appear only for the parental consent group where, as predicted, males are less likely to

TABLE 2
Discriminant Function Analysis of Participation*

Variable	Standardized Discriminant Function Coefficient	Canonical Correlation
Intelligence	−.005	
Grade Point	.438	
Type of Consent	.943	
Sex	.044	
		.293

*Using statistical procedures in Nie, et al., (1975).

return the consent forms. However, examination of the response percentages by grades and the base frequencies in the cells of the table show that this sex difference is largely a function of the relationship between sex and grade point. Grade point is related to participation in all but the lowest intelligence groups, although the relationship appears stronger in the parental consent group than in the student consent group. Interestingly enough, intelligence exhibits only a weak relationship to participation when grades and sex are both controlled.

Discriminant function analysis of the response groups presented in Table 2 shows the effects just described. Type of consent is by far the most important variable in the discriminating function, followed by grades. When grades are controlled, sex has very little effect while intelligence has almost no effect whatsoever.

The paramount influence of grade point and type of consent suggest apathy and irresponsibility may be behind student nonparticipation. For, given a sufficient aptitude, grades reflect motivation to conform to the demands of the school program. Viewing grades as an index of such motivation provides an explanation for the failure of the expected sex difference to occur when grades are included in the analysis. Grades are probably a better and more direct index of such conformity to school programs and purposes than is sex. The lower response of the parental consent group is consistent with a motivational explanation, for that procedure requires the student to be personally responsible and self-sufficient in a manner not required in the student consent procedure. Finally, an analysis (not reported here) of the interactions among these variables shows a complex interaction that can be observed in Table 1 in the stronger effect of grades among the males in the parental consent group, which increases with intelligence and culminates in the differences in the lower left hand cell, the largest of any cell in the table. It is among the parental consent males with high ability that external constraints on personal volition are minimized. These students have the ability to obtain whatever grades they choose, they play a sex role which emphasizes independence and nonconformity, and they are beyond the immediate control of the school regarding the return of the consent forms. The stronger relations between grades and participation in this cell is thus consistent with a motivational explanation of participation.

The idea that lack of motivation rather than objection to the study is the factor behind nonparticipation is also supported by casual observation of student reactions in the assembled survey administration groups. There appeared to be no overt objection to the study,[3] and it seemed that almost all of the students in the assembled groups did complete the questionnaire. We were able to document these impressions in two schools which used attendance lists of the students in the assembly. In these schools, all but four of the 412 students with adult status who attended the administration did return signed consent forms. Thus, there is no suggestion from these data that students perceived any harm in this research, nor had any serious objections to the study itself. It is also worth noting in this regard that as of the late summer of 1975, none of the parents of these 4770 students had communicated any complaint about the study to any of the school administrators.

The response rates in the individual schools varied widely from a low of 38% to a maximum of 95%. Reasoning that a school's ability to control its students through influence or coercion is a critical factor determining rate of participation, and that this control factor would probably be related to school size, we constructed the scattergrams shown in Figures 1 and 2, in which school size is operationalized as the number of students in the senior class. We were somewhat surprised to find the pronounced curvilinearity in the plot in Figure 1 which graphs participation in the student consent group by size.[4]

With the omission of school 9, (N = 414), which is an outlier,[5] a polynomial of the second order accounts for 81% of the variance in participation among the student consent groups in the remaining 17 high schools. (Even with school 9 included, the equation $Y = 104.79 - 2.92X + .0294X^2$ accounts for 64% of the variation in participation in the student consent group.)

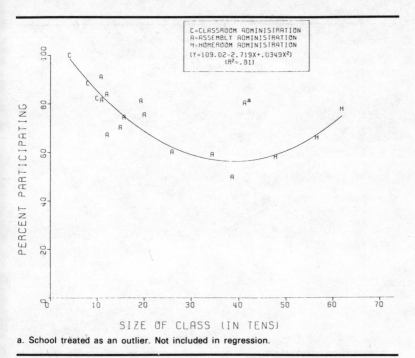

C=CLASSROOM ADMINISTRATION
A=ASSEMBLY ADMINISTRATION
H=HOMEROOM ADMINISTRATION
$(Y=109.02-2.719X+.0349X^2)$
$(R^2=.81)$

a. School treated as an outlier. Not included in regression.

Figure 1. Percentage Participating by Size of Class: Student Consent Group.

Examination of the detail in Figure 1 reveals that size of school is confounded with type of administration. In the three smallest schools, administrations were conducted in senior classes (C) and the rates of participation were high, although they did decline with size. In the majority of schools, survey administration was conducted in assemblies (A) and participation dropped off as size increased, with the notable exception of the outlier. Then, in the largest three schools, the surveys were administered in home rooms (H) with a resulting increase in participation.

The pattern in the home rooms and assembly administrations suggests the importance of size which we take to reflect processes of anonymity and identifiability and possibly also identification with and conformity to the purposes of the school administrations. The three classroom schools are almost exactly on a straight line (r = -.9997, p < .01). A linear regression also fits the 11 schools using assembly administration (r = -.8370, p < .01). Thus, within type of administration, increasing size means increasing inability of the school administrations to elicit cooperation and participation from their students.

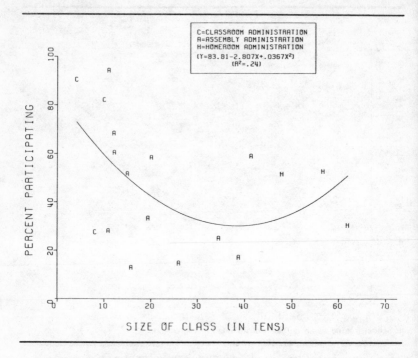

Figure 2. Percentage Participating by Size of Class: Parental consent Group.

These findings are consistent with the concept that anonymity reduces the effectiveness of social-control efforts.

The higher participation in the larger schools using home room administrations is also consistent with the idea of identifiability since home room sizes are between 20 and 35 students. The increasing participation over the three schools requires some other explanation. However, since this relationship is weak enough to have occurred by chance in a linear test (r = .9680, p $<$ .10) we will not speculate about it here.

Figure 2 shows that both size of school and type of administration have less to do with the rate of participation of students requiring parental consent. On the face of it, this seems consistent with our interpretation of Figure 1 as a school control process. Whatever control over the student the school might have established within the institution would presumably be less effective outside, and especially so where responsibility for action is shared to some degree with the parent. Figure 2 indicates that other things are operating to determine outcomes in the parental consent process. While we cannot explicate these other factors satisfactorily, our interpretations suggest that researchers face problems of institutional control in the student consent groups, but that they must deal with personal motivation as the major factor in the parental consent groups.

Response Bias

We now turn to an examination of the consequences of the non-response introduced by the informed-consent procedures. Following Cochran (1963), Rosenthal and Rosnow (1975), and Sewell and Hauser (1975) we define *bias* as the departure of an estimate based on the sample of participants from the population value. This is distinct from a *difference* which we define as the difference between participants and nonparticipants. In this section, we will investigate and report the amounts of bias and difference on five-known population parameters: the means and variances of both grade-point average and intelligence score, and the correlation between grade-point average and intelligence score. For each of these parameters, we shall ask two questions. First, is the bias (or the difference—the tests in each case are equivalent, though the values of the descriptive parameters are not) statistically significant? Second, regardless of the answer to that question, we shall be interested in the *amount* of the bias, most often expressed in standardized terms as the proportion of a standard deviation it represents, in a fashion similar to Rosenthal and Rosnow (1975) and Cohen (1969). We shall also present the coefficients of determination for the regression of the criterion variables on participation as another indicator of the magnitude of the bias introduced through nonparticipation.

Since several different intelligence tests were used in the several schools, and since there were some school-to-school differences in the way grade point average was represented, these two variables are expressed throughout the balance of this paper as standard scores within each school.[6]

Table 3 presents the different measures of bias for individual students in the total population and for the several consent subgroups. Of these ten comparisons, eight of the differences between participant and nonparticipant means are statistically significant.[7] The differences, however, are very small, and the biases, of course, are even smaller. The overall bias in grades is only .084 of a standard deviation while

TABLE 3
Bias in Grade Point and Intelligence

Participation Group	Males					
	Parental Consent			Student Consent		
	X	SD	N	X	SD	N
	(Grade Point)					
Participants	.099	.981	(273)	-.176	.977	(1038)
Nonparticipants	-.213	1.001	(453)	-.469	.916	(466)
Total	-.095	1.004	(726)	-.267	.968	(1504)
Difference (P-NP)	.312**	-.020		.293**	.061	
Bias (P-Total)	.194	-.023		.091	.009	
Standardized Bias (Bias/SD)	.193			.094		
r^2	.023**			.020**		
	(Intelligence)					
Participants	.270	.914	(262)	-.005	1.059	(964)
Nonparticipants	.158	.962	(418)	-.274	1.030	(426)
Total	.201	.945	(680)	-.088	1.057	(1390)
Difference (P-NP)	.112	-.048		.269**	.029	
Bias (P-Total)	.069	-.031		.083	.002	
Standardized Bias (Bias/SD)	.073			.078		
r^2	.003			.014**		

Participation Group	Females								
	Parental Consent			Student Consent			Total		
	X	SD	N	X	SD	N	X	SD	N
	(Grade Point)								
Participants	.469	.844	(410)	.198	.988	(950)	.084	.989	(2671)
Nonparticipants	.235	.973	(473)	-.054	.967	(395)	-.126	.999	(1787)
Total	.343	.922	(883)	.124	.988	(1345)	.000	.998	(4458)
Difference (P-NP)	.234**	-.129**		.252**	.021		.210**	-.010	
Bias (P-Total)	.126	-.078		.074	.000		.084	-.009	
Standardized Bias (Bias/SD)	.137			.075			.084		
r^2	.016**			.013**			.011**		
	(Intelligence)								
Participants	.228	.888	(394)	-.084	1.005	(888)	.032	1.008	(2508)
Nonparticipants	.068	.940	(440)	-.164	.925	(369)	-.049	.981	(1653)
Total	.144	.919	(834)	-.107	.982	(1257)	.000	.998	(4161)
Difference (P-NP)	.150*	-.052		.080	.090		.081**	.027	
Bias (P-Total)	.084	-.031		.023	.023		.032	.010	
Standardized Bias (Bias/SD)	.091			.023			.032		
r^2	.008**			.001			.002**		

*$p < .05$

**$p < .01$

that of intelligence is less than .04 of a standard deviation. Neither of these values is substantial, and both are much smaller than the value of .20 which Cohen (1969: 23-24) designates as a small effect. The coefficients of determination at the bottom of each panel of Table 3 throw further substantive meaning onto the bias values. In no case does the fact of participation or nonparticipation account for more than

2.3% of the variance in the variables of interest, and it accounts for only 1.1% of the variance in the total population for grade point and for only 0.2% of the variance in the total population for intelligence score. These values are surprisingly small given the overall participation rate of only 61%.

Table 3 also shows that there is neither substantively nor statistically significant bias in the variances of either variable in the total population. Among the consent subgroups, the two-tailed F-tests for homogeneity of variance show only one of the eight comparisons to be statistically significant, and even this difference is quite small. There does, however, appear to be a consistent pattern in the direction of the differences in variance across the consent groups. In the student consent groups the participants are more heterogeneous, while in the parental consent groups the nonparticipants are more heterogeneous. As these signs represent only one statistically significant difference, the pattern may not warrant speculation. However, it occurs to us that since the student consent group represents those in attendance and available for the survey, participants in this group may reflect the full range of student characteristics in the school. On the other hand, since parental consent group participation represents both characteristics of the attending students and also various off-campus influences, it is possible that the reasons for nonparticipation among the parental consent group might be varied enough to introduce greater heterogeneity than among the participants. That is, there may be more reasons for not returning the forms than for returning them.

Table 4 presents the results of the analysis of the relation between intelligence scores and grades, which we take as indicators of unspecified, but general student orientations toward school. Bias in the correlation coefficients in Table 4 are the differences between Fisher's logarithmic transformations of the correlations for the participants and those of the population (Snedecor and Cochran, 1967: 187). Cohen (1969: 75-76) argues that this difference is conceptually equivalent to the bias values of the means in Table 1. If that is so, the data in Table 3 are most encouraging. The biases (in terms of Fisher's z) are of the same small orders of magnitude as the biases in the means. Only two of the five differences between participant and nonparticipant correlations are statistically significant. However, none of the differences between the unstandardized regression coefficients of grade-point average on intelligence scores (McNemar, 1969: 161) for the participants and nonparticipants is significant, despite the fact that the values of the standardized and unstandardized coefficients are very close to each

TABLE 4
Bias in Correlation and Regression Between Intelligence Score and Grade Point Average.

Participation Group	Males						Females						Total		
	Parental Consent			Student Consent			Parental Consent			Student Consent					
	r	b	N	r	b	N	r	b	N	r	b	N	r	b	N
Participants	.67	.72	(262)	.62	.57	(964)	.60	.57	(394)	.64	.62	(888)	.61	.60	(2508)
Nonparticipants	.58	.60	(416)	.55	.49	(423)	.67	.69	(440)	.55	.57	(368)	.58	.59	(1647)
Total	.62	.65	(678)	.60	.55	(1387)	.64	.69	(834)	.61	.62	(1256)	.60	.60	(4155)
Difference (P-NP)[a]	.16*	.12		.10	.08		-.11	-.12		.14*	.05		.05	.01	
Bias (P-Total)[a]	.10	.07		.02	.02		-.04	-.12		.04	.00		.02	.00	

*p<.05, two-tailed test

a. Difference and bias of r's expressed in Fisher's z-units.

other, for reasons discussed above. Clearly then, the amount of bias in the grade point-intelligence correlation introduced by the informed-consent procedures is minor. Insofar as these correlations actually do index general student orientations toward the school program, these results have positive implications for the representativeness of the participant group on other educationally relevant variables not directly examined in this analysis.

Bias and the Rate of Participation

The final question in the analysis concerns the degree to which the small amount of bias we have observed can be explained by the rate of participation. By shifting our focus to the 18 individual schools, it will be possible to correlate the amount of bias in grade point, intelligence, and the correlation between them with the rate of participation. This analysis will provide evidence on the actual consequences of participation rate and also permit some rough evaluation of Babbie's (1973: 165) guidelines.

For this analysis we calculated the amount of bias on each of the two means and on the grade point-intelligence correlation within each school. Further, since a bias is a bias whether it is positive or negative, we took the absolute values of all of these figures. The resulting absolute-bias values for each school are plotted against participation rate in Figure 3. The appropriate mean values and correlations between the bias scores and rate of participation and between the bias measures themselves are presented in Table 5.

The results of this analysis show that response rate is not the important determinant of bias that we might assume it to be. In these 18 schools, the correlation between rate of participation and these measures of bias are −.47 for intelligence, −.26 for grade point, and −.12 for the intelligence grade point correlation. Only the largest of these is statistically significant.[8]

We must confess that we were surprised by the relatively low values of the correlations, but inspection of the scatterplots in Figure 3 indicates why they are so low. Heteroscedasticity is apparent in all three plots. There is little bias—and, of course, there cannot be extreme bias—in schools with high participation rates, but the amount of spread in the scatter tends to increase as the participation rate declines. This heteroscedasticity should serve as a warning to those inclined to use the results of this research to justify the use of samples with low

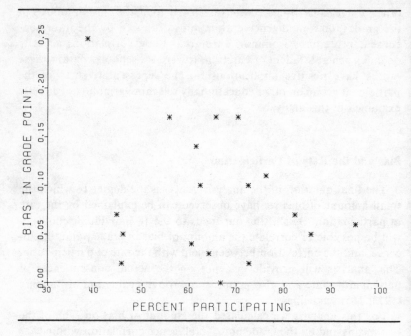

Figure 3.a. Bias in Grade Point by Percentage Participating.

response rates. It is possible that there would be little bias in the results of such an analysis even with very low response rates, but it is also possible that the bias would be more substantial. The researcher has no way of knowing. However, even though these data do not permit accurate prediction of bias from response rate, they do provide some support for Babbie's (1973: 165) rule of thumb that a response rate of 70% is "very good" for analysis and for the Sewell and Hauser (1975) conclusion that about 80% response rate is necessary to insure low bias. On the other hand, our data also show that once the response rate falls below 70% or 80%, heteroscedasticity makes response rate increasingly unimportant as a predictor of bias. In these data at least, below 70% anything can happen, and bias has little to do with the rate of response. It might be very low or it might be moderately high. We should reiterate, however, that the amount of bias is very small in all but one school.

Thus, the main finding of this analysis is that the bias that does exist cannot be predicted very well on the basis of response rate alone, but depends on other conditions of the sampling process as well. It is not possible to determine what these conditions are from these data, but

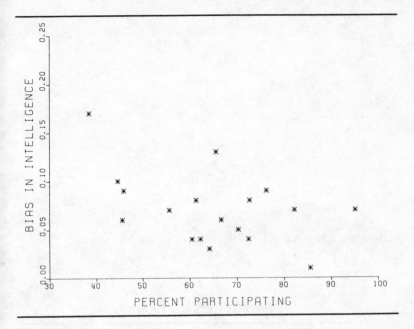

Figure 3.b. Bias in Intelligence by Percentage Participating.

whatever they are they must, of course, be correlated with the variables under study. Some reasons for low participation rates, such as field trips of whole classes, may not be selective of unique groups and may not produce bias, but others, such as lack of motivation, might well select unique groups and create bias. Our findings suggest that a concern with such patterns may be as (if not more) beneficial as exclusive concern with rate of response.

CONCLUSIONS AND DISCUSSION

This study has resulted in four main findings with implications for research. First, concerns about risk notwithstanding, we observed no strong objection to this study on the part of either students or their parents. Second, we found that voluntary participation and especially the use of parental consent procedures do reduce the rate of participation in survey research in high schools. However, we also found that the reduction in participation did not introduce serious bias. Finally, we found that rate of participation was only slightly

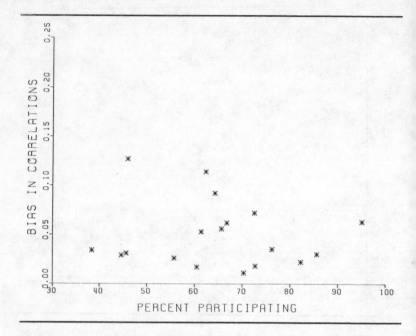

Figure 3.c. Bias in Grade Point-Intelligence Correlations by Percentage Participating.

correlated with the bias that was observed. A number of implications follow from these findings.

The lack of objection to this research by either students or parents indicates that the use of the involved informed-consent procedures with their attendant loss of cases was not absolutely necessary. In this case, we had the feeling students were being protected from a risk neither they nor their parents perceived. There is a real question in our minds whether in the absence of any actual or perceived risk, research projects such as this one should be handicapped by the additional cost and effort involved in carrying out informed-consent procedures.

The results of the data analysis have several implications for researchers. First, because there was essentially no refusal among adult students in attendance, the critical factor determining rate of participation of adult students is the assembly attendance itself. Both school size and size of the assembled group seem to be involved in determining rate of attendance. Because school size and the size of the survey assembly group are confounded in our data, it is impossible to clearly

TABLE 5
**Correlation Between Bias Measures and Percentage
Participating in Each of the Eighteen High Schools.**

	Percent Particip	Bias Measure		
		GPA	Intell	r GPA-Intell
Percentage Participating		-.26	-.47*	-.12
Bias in Grade Point			.59**	-.17
Bias in Intelligence				-.10
Mean	64.76	.090	.071	.050
SD	15.10	.067	.038	.034

*$p < .05$
**$p < .01$

separate the effects of these two variables. However, it seems reasonable to assume that the main factor is the size of the assembly itself (which is school size in most cases), probably because it determines the degree of anonymity that prevails. It is worth noting that size of the assembled group and student anonymity are factors which are to some degree under the control of the researcher and the school administrator. However, while school size is less important, the researcher should also recognize that our data indicate that the greatest problems of obtaining high rates of participation are likely to occur in medium and large-sized schools.

Second, it is clear that the parental consent procedure used in this study was not very effective. We had hoped that the minor students, having filled out the questionnaire, would be sufficiently interested in the project to return the forms, but this does not appear to have happened. A better approach would be to obtain follow-up actions and personal identifications of those students not returning the form. Considering that our experience suggests apathy, rather than objection, is the determining factor in nonreturn of these consent forms, requiring the return of the form for either consent or refusal would probably have increased the rate substantially.

Third, since response rate was not highly correlated with the amount of bias, the researcher might well direct his attention to the local conditions that may operate to produce bias in a particular school. While the factors that actually produced bias could not be determined in the present study, it is possible that consultation with school administrators prior to administration of questionnaires might provide insights into the local conditions likely to produce bias and permit the researcher to take special actions to counteract expected effects. Such efforts might be more fruitful in reducing the amount of bias than attempts to increase the rate of participation.

NOTES

1. The research on sex role change is being supported by grant MH26758 from the National Institute of Mental Health.

2. About 5% of the cases were lost because of mechanisms of administration. For example, some students appeared to be willing participants, but failed to transfer the coding number to the questionnaire as instructed, while others turned in a fully completed consent form with name and address but not signature. In two systems requiring a school board consent form, some students were lost to the study who signed and returned the survey consent form but failed to return the consent form required by the school board.

3. The only observed objection occurred in the larger schools where many students ridiculed or objected to the Coleman-inspired items requiring the rating of students who were "best athlete," "most popular," and so forth. We do not know whether these responses reflected defensiveness over ignorance of the school status structure or the espousal of egalitarian values. In any event, the same objections were rarely voiced in the smaller schools.

4. Both the linear and the quadradic terms in the polynomial regression equation given on the graph in Figure 1 are significant, but no terms of power greater than 2 were significant.

5. In this school, officials combined the survey administration with an effort to obtain signed consent forms for the school's local use of student records and transcripts. In accomplishing this, school 9 administered attendance forms signed by the students in the assembly and retained by the administration. All of the school counselors assisted the two professors in administering the questionnaires in this assembly. The result of these factors was a student rate of consent considerably above the level predicted. Statistical analysis indicates this school is in fact an outlier. A t-test for the difference betwen school 9's participation rate of 80.2% and its regression estimate of 53% (Walker and Lev, 1953: 400ff.), where the regression estimate is based on the second degree equation for the other 17 schools, yielded a t-value of 3.01 with 14 df (p .01).

6. For the total population, the grand means of the standard scores are zero and—perhaps fortuitously—the standard deviation on both variables are very near to unity. Thus, for all practical purposes, it would be redundant to restandardize the scores for the total population.

7. Significance is based upon two-tailed t-tests, employing in the two instances of nonhomogeneous variances, an approximation (Nie et al., 1975: 269-270).

8. The moderate effects of participation rate on bias in grades and intelligence compared to the negligible effect upon the correlation between them is consistent with Zetterberg's (1964) argument and Sewell and Hauser's (1975) finding that analytic research is more robust to problems of sample bias than descriptive research is.

9. Our experience is consistent with Sullivan's (1973) finding that professionals are more concerned about the protection of research subjects than are the subjects themselves.

REFERENCES

ALEXANDER, K. L., B. K. ECKLAND, and L. J. GRIFFEN (1975) "The Wisconsin model of socioeconomic achievement: a replication." Amer. J. of Sociology (September): 324-342.

American Sociological Association (1968) "Toward a code of ethics for sociologists." Amer. Sociologist 3 (November): 316-318.

BABBIE, E. R. (1973) Survey Research Methods. Belmont, CA: Wadsworth.

BAUMRIND, D. (1971) "Principles of ethical conduct in the treatment of subjects: reaction to the draft report of the Committee on Ethical Standards in Psychological Research." Amer. Psychologist 26: 887-896.

——— (1964) "Some thoughts on ethics of research after reading Milgram's 'Behavioral study of obedience.'" Amer. Psychologist 19 (June): 421-423.

CHASE, D. (1975) "No more 'brat' or 'bastards'." Nations's Schools and Colleges (January): 27-32.

COCHRAN, W. G. (1963) Sampling Techniques. New York: John Wiley.

COHEN, J. (1969) Statistical Power Analysis for the Behavioral Sciences. New York: Academic Press.

COLEMAN, J. (1961) The Adolescent Society. New York: Free Press.

CUTLER, M. (1975) "If the new student privacy law has you confused, perhaps that's because you're sane." Amer. School Board J. 162 (January): 44-49.

DAVIS, C. (1975) "The Buckley regulations: rights and restraints." Educational Researcher 4 (February): 11-13.

Department of Health, Education and Welfare (1975) "Protection of human subjects." 45 C.F.R.

DORN, D. S. and G. L. LONG (1974) "Brief remarks on the associations's code of ethics." Amer. Sociologist 9 (February): 31-35.

GALLIHER, J. F. (1973) "The protection of human subjects: a re-examination of the professional code of ethics." Amer. Sociologist 8 (August): 93-100.

GERGEN, K. J. (1973) "The codification of research ethics: views of a doubting Thomas." Amer. Psychologist 28 (October): 907-912.

KATZ, J. (1972) Experimentation with Human Beings. New York: Russell Sage.

KELMAN, H. C. (1972) "The rights of the subject in social research: an analysis in terms of relative power and legitimacy." Amer. Psychologist 27 (November): 989-1015.

——— (1965) "Manipulation of human behavior: an ethical dilemma for the social scientist." J. of Social Issues 21: 31-46.

McNEMAR, Q. (1969) Psychological Statistics. New York: John Wiley.

MILGRAM, S. (1964) "Issues in the study of obedience: a reply to Baumrind." Amer. Psychologist 19 (November): 848-852.

——— (1963) "Behavioral study of obedience." J. of Abnormal and Social Psychology 67 (October): 371-378.

NIE, N. H., C. H. HULL, J. G. JENKINS, K. STEINBRENNER, and D. H. BENT (1975) Statistical Package for the Social Sciences. New York: McGraw-Hill.

ROSENTHAL, R. and R. L. ROSNOW (1975) The Volunteer Subject. New York: John Wiley.

SEWELL, W. H. and R. M. HAUSER (1975) Education, Occupation and Earnings: Achievement in the Early Career. New York: Academic Press.

SNEDECOR, G. W. and W. G. COCHRAN (1967) Statistical Methods. Ames: Iowa State Univ. Press.

STEINER, I. D. (1972) "The evils of research: or what my mother didn't tell me about the sins of academia." Amer. Psychologist 27 (August): 766-768.

SULLIVAN, D. S. and T. E. BICKES (1973) "Subject-experimenter perceptions of ethical issues in human research." Amer. Psychologist 28 (July): 587-591.

SYKES, G. M. (1967) "Feeling our way: a report on a conference on ethical issues in the social sciences." Amer. Behavioral Scientist (June): 8-11.

VINACKE, W. E. (1954) "Deceiving experimental subjects." Amer. Psychologist 9 (April): 155.

WALKER, H. and J. LEV (1953) Statistical Inference. New York: Holt & Co.

WICKER, W. E. (1968) "Requirements for protecting privacy of human subjects: some implications for generalization of research findings." Amer. Psychologist 23 (January): 70-72.

ZETTERBERG, H. (1964) On Theory and Verification in Sociology, A Much Revised Edition. Totowa, NJ: Bedminister Press.

Lloyd B. Lueptow and Samuel A. Mueller are members of the Department of Sociology at the University of Akron. Professor Lueptow is presently completing a research project on change in adolescent sex roles from 1964 to 1975. Professor Mueller is coeditor of Sociological Focus *and has research interests in religion.*

Richard R. Hammes is Associate Professor in the College of Education, University of Wisconsin-Oshkosh where he is studying changes in student views about the functions of the high school.

Lawrence S. Master is a social studies consultant for the Keystone Area Education Agency of Dubuque, Iowa.

This paper provides a statistical method to analyze patterns of response to mail surveys. Based on the analysis of daily questionnaire returns, as recorded in 38 different social surveys which cover different subject matters, time periods, and populations surveyed, it is concluded that the patterns of response are relatively stable and can be statistically described by the gamma distribution. Based on this finding, researchers could forecast the patterns of response to mail surveys from the mean and variance of the distribution of daily questionnaire returns.

ANALYSIS OF PATTERNS OF
RESPONSE TO MAILED QUESTIONNAIRES

GIDEON VIGDERHOUS
Survey Research Group, Bell Canada

the general problem of analyzing patterns to mail surveys has received relatively little attention from survey analysts. The few studies conducted in this area (Lindsay, 1921; Robinson and Agisim, 1951; Gray, 1957; and Cox, 1966) are of a descriptive nature and do not examine the pattern of response to mail surveys beyond the elementary statistical level of analysis (graphic presentation, mean, coefficient of variation). These studies suggest that the response patterns of mailed questionnaires are stable and predictable.

The purpose of this paper is to provide a statistical method to analyze patterns of response to mail surveys. The major goal is to examine statistically the contention that response patterns to mailed surveys are stable and predictable. A secondary goal is to provide a statistical procedure to forecast anticipated response rates based on certain statistical assumptions. Statistical analysis of daily response rates will allow researchers to answer the following questions:

(a) How long should one wait before closing his survey?

(b) When should one start the call-back procedure in order to increase the response rate?

(c) Is there evidence that a very low or very high response rate may be anticipated based on questionnaire returns of the first few days, and so on?

AUTHOR'S NOTE: *The writer would like to thank Ted Speevak from the Management Sciences Division, Bell Canada, for his most valuable assistance in conducting this research.*

METHOD OF ANALYSIS

The major premise of the data analysis is that if patterns of response are relatively stable and predictable, then one can identify a statistical distribution that will be able to provide a good fit to the observed patterns of response. Thirty-eight different surveys, which provide statistics on daily returns of questionnaires, covering different subject matter, time periods, and populations surveyed are examined. Based on this analysis (see Table 1), it is concluded that the gamma distribution provides a good fit to patterns of response. The goodness of fit was determined by the statistical test of Kolmogorov-Smirnov (D[max]). Hence, a random variable t (time) is said to be distributed as the gamma distribution since it has the following function for its probability density:[1]

$$f(t; \alpha, \beta) \left\{ \frac{1}{\Gamma(\alpha)\beta^{\alpha}} \, t^{\alpha-1} e^{-t/\beta}, \, t > 0, \, \alpha, \beta > 0 \right. \qquad [1]$$

The parameters α and β determine the shape of the density function which is skewed to the right for all values of α and β. The skewness of the distribution decreases as α increases. The parameters α and β can be estimated directly from the mean and variance of the observed distribution:

$$\text{mean} = \alpha \beta$$
$$\text{variance} = \alpha \beta^2$$

Since the response patterns to mail surveys can be adequately described by the gamma distribution, we can obtain the value of t at which the density function attains its mode. In other words, a particular day of questionnaires returned can be identified in which the highest probability of questionnaires returned is observed.

The value of t at which the density function attains its mode can be derived by differentiating f(t; ,) and setting it equal to zero (see Appendix A1):

$$f^1(t; \alpha, \beta) = \frac{1}{(\alpha-1):\beta^{\alpha}} \left\{ (\alpha-1) t^{\alpha-2} e^{-(t/\beta)} - \frac{1}{\beta} t^{\alpha-1} e^{-(t/\beta)} \right\} = 0 \qquad [2]$$

It is found that $t = (\alpha - 1)\beta$. The value of t at the mode is obtained by substituting $\alpha - 1$ for in (1). The highest probability of questionnaire returns at the mode is derived by the following equation (see Appendix A2):

TABLE 1

Statistical Analysis of Response Pattern in Social Surveys by the Gamma Distribution

SURVEY NO.	SAMPLE SIZE	*NO. OF DAYS AFTER MAILING	RESPONSE RATE %	/' (BETA)	> (ALPHA)	MEAN	VARIANCE	MODE	PROBABILITY OF F(X) AT THE MODE	D (MAX)	PROBABILITY D (MAX)
1	305	17	59.01	2.2994	2.0343	4.6778	10.7559	2.3782	.1538	.1028	.0061
2	315	17	58.73	2.3153	2.4024	5.5622	12.8779	3.2469	.1358	.1341	.0803
3	459	16	60.13	1.6147	4.9748	8.0326	12.9698	6.0206	.1198	.0965	.0016
4	235	16	58.72	2.0119	2.8959	5.8261	11.7214	3.8139	.3669	.1392	.0840
5	319	17	55.79	2.6335	2.6944	6.7955	18.6857	4.4522	.1093	.1342	.0805
6	206	18	47.04	2.7306	2.4320	6.7133	18.5200	3.9515	.1336	.1520	.2003
7	188	16	64.36	1.8360	2.4480	6.3306	11.6231	4.4945	.1313	.1906	.3935
8	237	17	61.60	2.4995	2.7951	6.9863	17.4619	4.4869	.1120	.1582	.2115
9	840	17	66.80	2.0578	3.6293	7.4685	15.3689	5.4107	.1144	.1602	.2242
10	853	16	54.22	2.2520	3.1364	7.0632	15.9065	4.8112	.1159	.1840	.3492
11	261	17	49.80	2.9736	2.0048	5.9615	17.7272	2.9880	.1229	.1474	.1463
12	475	17	58.94	2.9901	2.2419	6.7036	20.0444	3.7135	.1113	.1599	.1918
13	294	17	51.36	3.5549	1.5127	5.3775	19.1166	1.8226	.1339	.2054	.5297
14	367	17	45.50	3.1219	1.9488	6.0838	18.9929	2.9620	.1199	.1745	.3215
15	518	17	48.45	3.4552	1.7573	6.0717	20.9788	2.6165	.1181	.1907	.4333
16	1525	17	59.86	2.2644	3.1125	7.0481	15.9604	2.7835	.1159	.0968	.0048
17	1563	22	32.37	2.8980	3.9573	11.4684	33.2356	8.5703	.0077	.0850	.0101
18	2645	19	60.00	2.1325	3.5393	7.5476	16.0953	5.4150	.1123	.1610	.2962
19	1915	17	51.12	3.1615	2.0303	6.4188	20.2927	3.2573	.1140	.1448	.1318
20	912	20	45.72	3.0870	1.6376	5.0552	15.6051	1.9682	.1421	.1750	.4270
21	889	19	52.30	3.6764	1.7163	6.3097	23.1920	2.6334	.1137	.1668	.3659
22	632	19	48.41	3.5927	1.6064	5.7712	20.7344	2.1786	.1243	.1304	.0970
23	672	20	54.01	3.0535	2.1011	6.4160	19.5917	3.3622	.1143	.1468	.2183
24	559	21	58.49	2.8036	2.6058	7.2058	20.4829	4.5022	.1054	.1471	.2458
25	3664	21	51.25	2.8418	2.5077	7.1262	20.2510	4.2846	.1075	.1599	.3434
26	3976	18	69.99	1.6279	2.9431	4.7909	7.8988	3.1231	.1716	.1183	.0459
27	5864	19	70.00	1.4556	3.3884	4.9338	9.1805	3.3287	.1506	.2134	.6474
28	1993	18	81.00	1.5366	3.3566	5.1832	7.5963	3.7176	.1632	.1499	.1867
29	1993	16	72.00	1.7542	2.5989	4.5589	7.9971	2.8040	.1689	.0962	.0016
30	1991	19	75.99	1.4359	3.2460	4.6609	6.6925	3.2250	.1758	.1819	.4440
31	2997	19	64.99	2.2502	2.5510	5.7403	12.9166	3.4900	.1318	.1823	.4824
32	4976	17	67.00	1.8553	3.4031	6.3137	11.7137	4.4585	.1314	.2385	.7118
33	3003	17	73.99	2.1957	2.7096	5.9496	13.0636	3.7538	.1263	.2399	.7181
34	1003	17	67.00	1.6638	3.1079	5.1709	8.6032	3.5071	.1550	.1230	.1561
35	3000	26	84.50	4.6973	1.5995	7.5130	35.2906	2.8160	.0959		
36	3000	15	74.60	2.4140	2.3835	5.7538	13.8897	3.3970	.1306	.1667	.2014
37	2000	27	93.85	5.1164	1.3567	6.9414	35.5154	1.8250	.1058	.1473	.3748
38	2000	15	81.55	2.6876	1.9578	5.2618	14.1418	2.5741	.1372	.1863	.3249

The data for surveys 1-25 were collected by the Survey Research Group.
The data for surveys 26-34 were obtained from Robinson & Agisim (1951).
The data for surveys 35-38 were obtained from Gray (1957).
*The number of days after mailing are counted since the return of the first questionnaire(s).

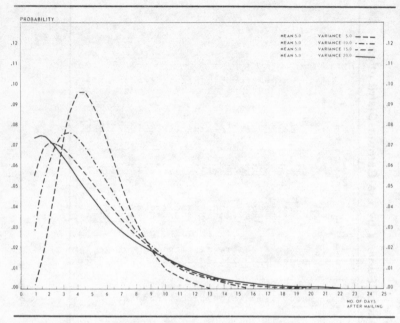

Figure 1: Daily Probabilities of Questionnaire Returned

$$f(t) = \frac{(\alpha-1)^{(\alpha-1)} e^{-(\alpha-1)}}{\Gamma(\alpha)\beta} \qquad [3]$$

Table 1 presents the relevant statistics of the analyzed daily questionnaire returns of 38 social surveys.[2] From this table it can be learned that the patterns of response to social surveys are relatively stable since in all instances the empirical distribution is not significantly different from the theoretical gamma distribution. In order to reject the null hypothesis that there is no difference between the observed and expected distribution for n = 17, the D(max) value should be greater than .318 for 5% level of significance. Similarly, the probability of D(max) should be greater than .80. From examination of the α and β parameters, it can be observed that the values will vary from one survey to the other. It may be observed that the mean value (number of questionnaires returned by day) is relatively stable; however, the variance will vary considerably from one survey to the other. An interesting result from this analysis is that the mode and its probability are stable. This suggests that, on the average, the highest probability of questionnaire returns for a single day is obtained on the fourth day from the first return.

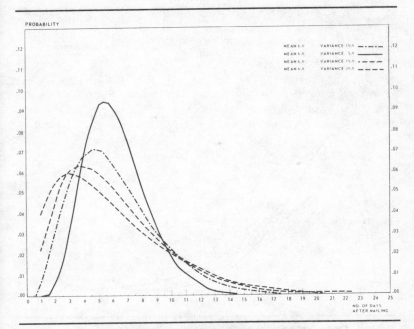

Figure 2: Daily Probabilities of Questionnaire Returned

The empirical evidence that the pattern of response to mailed questionnaires which can be described by the gamma distribution can be utilized to construct a profile of response patterns. Figure 1 represents the hypothetical daily probabilities of the questionnaires returned when the mean is held constant $\overline{X} = 5.0$ and the variance between 5.0-20.0. From this figure it can be learned when each distribution reaches its maximum probability of questionnaires returned for a single day.

Figure 2 represents the daily probabilities of questionnaires returned when the mean was increased to $\overline{X} = 6.0$ and the variance (σ^2) varies as before between 5.0-20.0. A shift in the mode values or the maximum probability of questionnaires returned for a single day can be observed when compared to Figure 1. Generally, the higher the mean, the longer is the waiting time (in days) to observe the maximum probability of questionnaires returned when the variance is held constant.

Figure 3 represents the pattern of response of surveys 1-25 (see Table 1). The profile is based on the mean of means questionnaire returns per day -6.656 and the mean of the variances 17.939. The parameters for this distribution are $\alpha = 2.5507$ and $\beta = 2.6095$. From this figure it can be seen

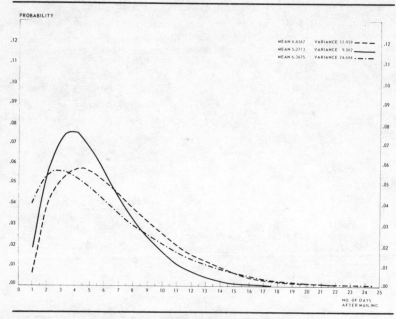

Figure 3: Daily Probabilities of Questionnaire Returned

that the highest probability is observed for t = 4 which is the fourth day from the first returns.[3] The fact that the response pattern constitutes an asymmetrical distribution suggests that with respect to time (t) the mode will be observed first, then the median, and the mean. Similarly, the profile of patterns of response for surveys 26-34 and 36-38 are calculated (Figure 3).

HOW TO FORECAST QUESTIONNAIRE RETURNS

In order to forecast questionnaire returns, the following information is required: (1) the mean value of questionnaire returns per day, (2) the variance of questionnaire returns, and (3) the overall estimation of response rate.

(1) The mean value can be estimated from the observed distribution even though there are only a few observations. However, it is desirable to compare this mean value to values obtained in past surveys.

TABLE 2
Estimated Probabilities of Questionnaire Returns*

NUMBER OF DAYS**	PROBABILITIES	CUMULATIVE PROBABILITIES	CUMULATIVE RETURNS
1	0.0868	0.0868	52
2	0.1395	0.2262	136
3	0.1415	0.3677	221
4	0.1272	0.4949	297
5	0.1080	0.6029	362
6	0.0885	0.6914	415
7	0.0709	0.7623	457
8	0.0507	0.8183	491
9	0.0436	0.8619	517
10	0.0336	0.8955	537
11	0.0258	0.9213	553
12	0.0196	0.9409	565
13	0.0149	0.9558	573
14	0.0112	0.9670	580
15	0.0084	0.9754	585
16	0.0063	0.9817	589
17	0.0047	0.9864	592
18	0.0035	0.9899	594
19	0.0027	0.9926	596
20	0.0019	0.9945	597

*The probabilities were derived from the gamma distribution based on the following statistical assumptions: $\overline{X} = 5$, $\sigma^2 = 15$, $N = 1000$ and 60% response rate.
**The number of days since the return of the first questionnaire(s).

(2) The variance cannot be efficiently estimated from a few observations, therefore, one should assume its value. Again, the accuracy of the assumption will depend on the variance observed in past similar surveys.

(3) The overall response rate is required in order to translate the probability values into actual forecasted questionnaire returns. Given that mean and variance are given or assumed, one can construct the overall distribution of daily response rates. The parameter α can be estimated also from β and the mode value as follows:

$$\beta = \frac{\text{variance}}{\text{mean}} \qquad \alpha = \frac{\text{mode}}{\beta} + 1.0$$

The following example presents the forecast for a survey of mean value 5.0 and estimated variance of 15.0. It is assumed that the overall response rate is 60% where the number of questionnaires mailed out is $N = 1000$. Table 2 presents the probabilities of questionnaire returns and the estimated cumulative questionnaire return by day.

WHEN TO START THE CALL-BACK PROCEDURE
TO INCREASE THE RESPONSE

It may be suggested that the call-back procedure which intends to increase the response rate should be started when the probabilities of questionnaire returns is significantly small. These probabilities can be observed from the gamma distribution. For example, based on the probabilities calculated on the profile of response patterns (Figure 1), it may be suggested that the call-back procedure should take place between the twelfth and fifteenth day from the first returns.

By adopting this approach to the call-back procedure, the following results may be obtained:

(a) the probability of calling back a respondent who might send his questionnaire without reminder will be minimized;

(b) the waiting time for completing the survey after the reminder procedure will be minimized.

It may also be suggested that the longer the time elapsed between mailing the first questionnaire and the reminder, the less effective is the reminder itself (the individual might forget that he received a questionnaire or he might lose it).

SUMMARY

This paper demonstrates that the patterns of response to mailed questionnaires can be statistically described by the gamma distribution. Based on this evidence, a forecast of daily questionnaire returns may be established from the mean and variance of the empirical distribution. Examination of the daily probabilities of questionnaire returns may assist in conducting an effective call-back procedure and in minimizing the waiting time for the completion of the survey. This would contribute to the solution of budgetary and timing problems in mail surveys.

NOTES

1. $$\Gamma\,(\alpha) = \int_0^\infty x^{\alpha-1}\,e^{-x}\,dx.$$

2. In order to find the probability of questionnaire returns for a given day (t) the function f(t) was integrated as follows:

$$P(t) = \int_{t-.05}^{t+.05} f(t)$$

3. The probability of questionnaire returns at the mode (t = 4) was estimated as .11954.

REFERENCES

COX, W. E. Jr. (1966) "Response patterns to mail surveys." J. of Marketing Research 3 (November): 392-393.

GRAY, P. G. (1957) "A sample survey with both a postal and an interview stage." Applied Statistics 6 (June): 139-153.

LINDSAY, E. E. (1921) "Questionnaires and follow-up letters." Pedagogical Seminary 28 (September): 303-307.

ROBINSON, R. A. and P. AGISIM (1951) "Making mail surveys more reliable." J. of Marketing 15 (April): 415-424.

Gideon Vigderhous is a Surveys Analyst at Bell Canada, where he conducts research in the areas of public relations, corporate performance, advertising, and the application of quantitative techniques to survey problems.

APPENDIX A

PART 1

$$f(t) = \frac{1}{\Gamma(\alpha)\beta^{\alpha}} t^{\alpha-1} e^{-t/\beta}, \; t>0, \alpha>0, \beta>0$$

$$\frac{d[f(t)]}{dt} = \frac{1}{\Gamma(\alpha)\beta^{\alpha}} [(\alpha-1) t^{\alpha-2} e^{-t/\beta} + t^{\alpha-1} e^{-t/\beta}(-\frac{1}{\beta})]$$

Critical points occur when $\iff \dfrac{d[f(t)]}{dt} = 0$

Solving for critical points:

$$\frac{1}{\Gamma(\alpha)\beta^{\alpha}} [(\alpha-1)t^{\alpha-2} e^{-t/\beta} + t^{\alpha-1} e^{-t/\beta}(-\frac{1}{\beta})] = 0$$

multiplying both sides by $\dfrac{\Gamma(\alpha)\beta^{\alpha}}{e^{-t/\beta}}$, yields

$$(\alpha-1)t^{\alpha-2} + t^{\alpha-1}(-\frac{1}{\beta}) = 0$$

$$t^{(\alpha-2)}(\alpha-1 - \frac{1}{\beta}t) = 0$$

Since $t \neq 0$

$$\Rightarrow \frac{1}{\beta}t = \alpha-1$$

and $t = (\alpha-1)\beta = \alpha\beta - \beta$

PART 2

Value of f(t) a the mode:

$$f(t) = \frac{1}{\Gamma(\alpha)\beta^{\alpha}} t^{(\alpha-1)} e^{-t/\beta} = \frac{1}{\Gamma(\alpha)\beta^{\alpha}} [(\alpha-1)\beta]^{\alpha-1} e^{-(\alpha-1)}$$

$$= \frac{(\alpha-1)^{\alpha-1} \beta^{\alpha-1}}{\Gamma(\alpha)\beta^{\alpha}} e^{-(\alpha-1)} = \frac{(\alpha-1)^{(\alpha-1)}}{\Gamma(\alpha)\beta} e^{-(\alpha-1)}$$

Procedures for treating missing data in the statistical analysis of survey data are reviewed. The main topics covered are: (1) how to assess the nature of missing data especially with regard to randomness, (2) a comparison of listwise and pairwise deletion, and (3) methods for using maximum information to estimate (a) parameters or (b) missing values.

THE TREATMENT OF MISSING DATA IN
MULTIVARIATE ANALYSIS

JAE-ON KIM
JAMES CURRY
University of Iowa

for any large data set it is unlikely that complete information will be present for all the cases. In surveys which rely on respondents' reports of behavior and attitudes, it is almost certain that some information is either missing or in an unusable form. Although statisticians have long appreciated that the existence of such missing information can change an ordinarily simple statistical analysis into a complex one (e.g., Orchard and Woodbury, 1972) and responded to this challenge by producing enormous amounts of literature (see, for example, Afifi and Elashoff, 1966; Hartley and Hocking, 1971; Orchard and Woodbury, 1972; Press and Scott, 1974), there is little indication that survey researchers have paid much attention to the literature. When faced with such missing-data problems, most survey researchers are likely to choose either a listwise deletion or pairwise deletion, and then proceed to interpret the resulting statistics as usual.[1]

The primary objective of this paper is to review and organize the procedures for handling missing data, having in mind the practical needs of survey researchers with a relatively complex analysis problem but with little statistical sophistication. To make the task manageable, we will confine our discussion mostly to the situation in which variables are measured at least on an interval scale. Other situations will be dealt with only when such excursion is simple and does not interrupt the flow of the presentation. For researchers with specific problems not discussed in this paper, a brief bibliographical note is included.

MISSING DATA PROBLEMS:
A PRACTICAL OVERVIEW

There are many different ways to categorize the treatment of missing data problems. From the practical point of view, however, the most important question is when and under what conditions can one safely consider the problem of missing information to be trivial. This much is obvious: the smaller the relative proportion of missing information, the larger the sample, and the more random the missing information, the less troublesome the missing data problems.

If the sample size is large, as is usually the case in survey research, and the proportion of missing data relatively small, probably the first options to consider for handling missing data are the simplest ones: listwise deletion or pairwise deletion. If the problem can be handled safely by either of these options, the missing-data problem may be considered trivial. But when is the proportion of missing data considered relatively small? The overall loss of data for a given analysis depends on several factors: the proportion of missing observations on each variable, the number of variables under consideration, the degree to which missing observations are clustered, and the choice of procedures for handling missing data.

Although listwise deletion is the simplest, there is an inherent conflict in the often recommended requirements for its use in that for a fixed number of variables and a given proportion of missing cases for each variable, the number of deleted cases increases as the pattern of missing information becomes more random. To illustrate, if only 2% of the cases contain missing values on each variable and the pattern of missing values is random, the listwise procedure will delete 18.3% of the cases in an analysis using 10 variables. As the overlap of missing values increases, the loss due to listwise deletion will decrease, in the extreme to 2% of the cases. Pairwise deletion is an attractive alternative when the number of missing cases on each variable is small relative to the total sample size, the pattern of missing values is random, and the number of variables involved is large.

The problem with the use of listwise deletion is the relatively greater loss of data, whereas the problem with the pairwise deletion is the potential inconsistency of the covariance matrix in a multivariate context.[2] There is an approach which tries to overcome the limitations of these two simple procedures. The basic strategy of this approach is to estimate in the first step the missing *values* (not parameters) from the available information and then proceed to the estimation of parameters. The drawback of this approach is that except for very simple situations it depends on iterative numerical solutions, making it out of reach of most survey researchers (at least until ready-made computer programs are more widely available.) But the advantages of this approach are too compelling not to consider its adoption: (1) the parameter estimation is more efficient because a greater amount of available information is used and (2) it allows at the same time the use of estimated values for index construction, thereby preventing a severe data loss in complex analyses.

Keeping in mind, however, the varied needs of researchers, we will organize our discussion around the following three practical issues: (1) how to evaluate whether or not observations are randomly missing and how to live with a potentially serious missing data problem, (2) if missing data are trivial, what are the factors to consider in choosing between listwise and pairwise deletion, and (3) when these simpler methods are inappropriate what are the general techniques available in the literature.

ASSESSING THE NATURE OF MISSING DATA

Almost all the techniques suggested in the literature assume that information is missing randomly (see Buck, 1960; Hartley and Hocking, 1971; Orchard and Woodbury, 1972; Beale and Little, 1974). But the simple dichotomy—random versus nonrandom—is often not sufficient. We begin therefore with a brief examination of various patterns of missing data.

TYPES OF MISSING DATA

Because the most important aspect of missing data is whether and to what extent the missing information may be considered random, the following categorization is chiefly based on the pattern of randomness.

(1) Missing data is randomly produced. That is, whether information is missing or not on a given variable is unrelated to the values of that variable or to the values of other variables in the data set. As the sample size increases, it is expected not only that the mean and variance of each variable and the covariance between any two variables will be affected less by the existence of missing data but

also that the pattern of missing data will exhibit such randomness. By the pattern of missing data we mean the frequency distribution of different categories of missing patterns such as missing only on X_1, missing on both X_1 and X_2, and so on.

(2) Missing data on a given variable X_1 is dependent on the value of another variable X_2. The differentiating characteristic of this pattern is whether information is missing on a given variable X_1 is not dependent on the value of X_1 but rather on its underlying relationship with another variable X_2. Therefore, whether or not information is missing on X_1 is independent of the values of X_1 given values of X_2. This represents an important class of missing data which is not completely random but allows simple factorization of maximum likelihood (e.g., see Little, 1976a; 1976b). An example of this type of missing data problem can be found in the situation in which respondents are asked whether they voted in previous elections but some were ineligible to vote because of age.[3] Or, in a panel study, a whole set of information may be missing from the later waves for some respondents who were not available. The missing data pattern will be systematic, but the cause of the missing data may be independent of the values of the variables under consideration (Rubin, 1976).

(3) Underlying values not observed in a given data set may determine whether information is missing or not. For example, in an attitudinal survey, a respondent with low cognitive skills may refuse or be unable to give usable answers to many questions. In this case, the pattern of missing data will exhibit clustering. The difference between this case and (2) above is that here the variable which determines the pattern of missing data is not included in the survey. The practical difference is that in case (2) the missing information can be made conditionally independent of its underlying values by controlling for the differences in the determining factor (e.g., age). Such a control is usually impossible in the present example. But the difference between cases (2) and (3) is not an absolute one; there may exist variables such as education and other measures of cognitive ability with which the underlying syndrome may be approximated and factored out.

(4) Whether information is missing on a given variable X_1 is dependent on the values of itself, that is, X_1. For example, respondents with excessively high income may be reluctant to reveal their level of income. In this type of missing data problem, the mean and variance of the variable is affected by the existence of missing information. The degree to which the missing information can be estimated from the existing data will depend on the degree to which the variable is related to other variables in the data set, but unless the determination

is complete, completely eliminating the effects of missing data is not possible. In addition, an examination of the pattern of missing data alone may not provide clues to the nature of this type of missing data.

(5) Missing data is a product of a particular combination of two or more variables. For instance, people with *high* education may be less inclined to reveal their *low* income, or people with high income may be unwilling to reveal their low education. In this type of situation, any effort to recover the missing information from the relationship between the variables in existing data would be misleading.

TESTING FOR A RANDOM PATTERN

A simple test for the randomness of missing values can be devised if missing values are relatively large and many variables are involved in the analysis. The strategy is to consider the $(K + 2)$ patterns of missing data where K is the number of variables with a substantial number of missing cases (say, 20 or over). The pattern to consider is: (M_1), (M_2), . . . (M_k), (MM—missing on two or more variables), and (NM—none missing) where M_i stands for cases on which information is missing only on the variable X_i. To illustrate, if there are three variables, X_1, X_2, and X_3, the categories involved and the expected frequencies under the assumption of randomness are given as follows:

$$M_1 = (Q_1 P_2 P_3)N$$
$$M_2 = (Q_2 P_1 P_3)N$$
$$M_3 = (Q_3 P_2 P_3)N$$
$$MM = (1 - P_1 P_2 P_3) N - M_1 - M_2 - M_3$$
$$NM - (P_1 P_2 P_3)N$$

where Q_i and P_i stand respectively for the proportion of missing and nonmissing cases of variable i. The significance of the deviation of the observed frequencies from the expected frequencies can be evaluated by the ordinary χ^2 test with degrees of freedom equal to the $(K + 1)$ number of variables involved.[4]

If such tests indicated that the missing data can be assumed random, then many techniques suggested in the literature are available. In particular, the adoption of either pairwise or listwise deletion may be seriously considered. But it should be noted that this test is of no use if missing information exists on only one variable or there is nonrandomness such that (as in case [5]) the examination of the pattern alone is not sufficient.

USE OF INDICATOR VARIABLES

As suggested by Cohen and Cohen (1975), it is convenient to represent the existence of missing data with dummy indicator variables. Following their lead, we will illustrate the use of indicator variables in the context of bivariate regression. They argue that in a (bivariate) regression it is convenient to delete cases with missing information on the dependent variable (Y) from the analysis. If one follows their suggestion, one will have the following simple pattern of missing data:

$$Y: y_1 \, y_2 \ldots y_m \, y_{m+1} \, y_{m+2} \ldots y_n$$
$$X: x_1 \, x_2 \ldots x_m$$

(Pattern A)

We assume that cases are rearranged such that cases missing on the independent variable (X) are placed at the end so that $m < N$.

If the missing information on X is missing randomly, we would expect that the mean of Y for the first m cases would be similar to the mean of Y for the last $(N - m)$ cases. The simplest way to test whether such an expectation is met in the data is to create a dummy indicator variable X_a (assigning 1 if the information is missing and O otherwise) and then regress Y on X_a. The constant a in the regression equation $Y = a + bX_a$ will represent the mean of Y for the first m (compete) cases and the coefficient b will represent the difference between the mean of the missing cases and that of the nonmissing cases. The test for the significance of b will serve as a test for the randomness of the missing data.

Furthermore, if one inserts any arbitrary constant in the place of the missing X values and regresses Y on both X and X_a, then the partial regression coefficient associated with X will be equivalent to the simple b that would be obtained from the complete data of the m cases. The data pattern would then be:

$$Y: y_1 \, y_2 \ldots\ldots\ldots\ldots\ldots\ldots\ldots\ldots\ldots\ldots\ldots\ldots\ldots\ldots\ldots\ldots y_n$$
$$X: x_1 \, x_2 \ldots\ldots\ldots\ldots\ldots\ldots\ldots\ldots x_n \, c \, c \ldots\ldots\ldots c$$
$$X_a: 0 \, 0 \ldots\ldots\ldots\ldots\ldots\ldots\ldots\ldots 0 \, 1 \, 1 \ldots\ldots\ldots 1$$

The increment in R^2 due to X from the dummy regression is equivalent to the simple r^2 that would exist for the first m cases. The complete analysis calls for a hierarchical regression. If, on the other hand, the missing values on X are replaced by the mean of X (for the m cases), then the regression of Y on X and X_a need not be made in a hierarchical fashion; the partial b's associated with X and X_a are then equivalent to simple b's (see Cohen and Cohen, 1975, for more illustrations and uses of different coding methods).

The use of dummy indicator variables can be easily extended to the situation in which X is a categorical variable. The only adjustment necessary is to regress Y on the missing data indicator variable X_a first and then on both X_a and other dummy variables representing (K – 1) categories of X. Cohen and Cohen therefore argue that it is not only unnecessary to assume randomness in missing data but also unwise to do so when such easy means of handling missing data are available (1975: 288).

It must be noted, however, that their suggestion is of limited value in most survey research where many variables are examined in a complex manner as in path analysis. In path analysis, a variable is often considered a dependent variable in one context, but an independent variable in another context. Nevertheless, the use of a dummy indicator variable is very convenient in testing whether the type (4) situation exists. If information is missing on Y because of the underlying values of Y itself (type [4]), one would look for another variable (Z) that is closely related to Y. Then one would regress Z on Y_a (the indicator variable) and test whether the b associated with Y_a is significant. One must be cautious, however, in interpreting a result from such a bivariate case. Even if the missing cases have different means on some variables, it does not mean that the pattern belongs to case (4); the case (2) can produce significant differences if the bivariate association between the two variables is strong. As will be shown later, such situations can be exploited as means of obtaining extra information about the missing data.

Another method suggested by Cohen and Cohen (1975: 286f) is to examine the relationships among the missing data indicator variables to see if there is any significant clustering. Although applying factor analysis to dichotomous variables is not fully justified, such an application may still provide means of identifying important underlying dimensions of the clustering of missing values when the correlations are moderate (Kim et al., 1977). Such examination of clustering may help identify the underlying causes of missing data. Even if the nature of missing data remains obscure, one can at least control for the unknown effects of missing data more efficiently by including missing value scales along with other independent variables in a multivariate analysis (Cohen and Cohen, 1975: 286f.).

An examination of the correlation matrix for the set of missing-data indicator variables can also serve as a quick way of ascertaining whether there is any unusual clustering between missing values of two variables. Noting that the correlation between dichotomous variables (r_{ij}) is equivalent to ϕ, and that $\phi^2 = \chi^2/N$, one may consult the χ^2 table with $\chi^2 = \phi^2$ (N) and degrees of freedom = 1 (Cramer, 1946: 441-445).[5]

As may have been obvious from the discussion in this section, the researcher really does not have much recourse in assessing the nature of the missing data. The final assessment should be based on substantive knowledge about the content and the circumstances under which the data were collected.

LISTWISE AND PAIRWISE DELETION

If one is willing to assume (or the test for randomness shows) that the pattern of missing data does not deviate significantly from the random model, the easiest options to consider are listwise and pairwise deletion of missing cases.

As noted earlier, the disadvantage of listwise deletion is the relatively greater loss of data. Its advantages are that it always generates consistent covariance and correlation matrices and that test statistics used with the complete data can be used without modification. The advantages and disadvantages of pairwise deletion are complementary to those of listwise deletion. The matrix generated by pairwise deletion may not be consistent (not positive-definite), especially when the missing data pattern is not random or when the total sample size is small.[6] Furthermore, the sampling distribution of estimates based on pairwise deletion usually contains nuisance parameters which are not readily computable (Haitovsky, 1968).

The choice between the two methods, even in trivial situations, is not clearly indicated in the literature. Using the matrix based on pairwise deletion may be close to the spirit of maximum likelihood solutions proposed for missing data problems (e.g., see Haitovsky, 1968; for a summary of earlier literature of maximum likelihood solutions, see Anderson, 1957). A specific comparison between the two methods was first attempted (as far as we know) by Buck (1960) in his examination of several methods for handling missing data. He compared the estimated coefficients using various methods of handling missing data to those based on the complete (74 cases) data (Buck, 1960: 305). Among other things, he showed that listwise deletion produced results closer to the complete data than pairwise deletion. Because his conclusion is based on the examination of a single data set (containing 72 cases and 4 variables from which he randomly deleted a few cases from each variable resulting in a total loss of 34 cases) and *a single* simulation, his conclusion should not be taken seriously.

Glasser (1964) argued that the efficiency of pairwise deletion over listwise deletion improves as the overall correlation among the independent variables decreases, and may become better when the sample is large and correlations are below a certain level, given a fixed pattern of missing values. For example, for the situation where there are two independent variables and the proportion of missing values is uniform, the efficiency of estimating partial b's from the covariance matrix based on the pairwise deletion is in general better than that based on the listwise deletion if the magnitude of correlation between the two variables is less than .58 (Glasser, 1964: 839).

As far as we know, Haitovsky (1968), through the use of computer simulation, has performed the most systematic and extensive comparisons between the two methods. His finding is fairly conclusive: listwise deletion is in general superior to pairwise deletion in the estimation of partial regression coefficients. He summarizes his finding as follows: "In almost all the cases which were investigated the former method [ordinary least squares applied only to complete observations] is judged superior. However, when the proportion of incomplete observations is high or when the pattern of the missing entries is highly non-random, it seems plausible that one of the many methods of assigning values to the missing entries should be applied" (Haitovsky, 1968: 67). Later publications based on simulations do not consider the pairwise deletion partly on the basis of evidence presented by Haitovsky (e.g., Timm, 1970; Beale and Little, 1974).

After carefully examining Haitovsky's simulation model, however, we conclude that he does not have a model typical of sociological data, which usually contains only moderate bivariate correlations and a multiple R usually not beyond .7. Furthermore, it is not clear at what point the proportion of missing observations should be considered to be high. Partly for these reasons, we have made our own simulations using Blau and Duncan's correlation matrix among status-attainment variables as the model (Blau and Duncan, 1967: 169).

More specifically, we have simulated sampling 1,000 cases from a multivariate-normal population with a correlation matrix equal to Blau and Duncan's matrix, and we deleted randomly about 10% of the cases from each variable.[7] Such sampling was repeated 10 times, and the resulting sample correlations and covariance matrixes were compared with the population model. The results are present in Table 1.

TABLE 1

Simulation Results, Using Blau-Duncan's Correlation Matrix as the Model, Sample of 1000, Replicated 10 Times, from Multivariate Normal Population, and 10% of Cases are made Missing Randomly from Each Variable

| | | Mean Deviation from the Model | | | |
| | | Correlations | | Covariances | |
	Blau-Duncan Model	List-Wise Deletions	Pair-Wise Deletions	List-Wise Deletions	Pair-Wise Deletions
YW	.541	.0285	.0248	.0453	.0331
YU	.596	.0320	.0202	.0548	.0369
YX	.405	.0311	.0272	.0418	.0366
YV	.322	.0266	.0271	.0306	.0327
WU	.538	.0259	.0223	.0436	.0379
WX	.417	.0228	.0203	.0267	.0263
WV	.332	.0354	.0334	.0526	.0452
UX	.438	.0355	.0254	.0540	.0386
UV	.453	.0287	.0279	.0447	.0378
XV	.516	.0292	.0262	.0460	.0424
Overall Deviation Index		.0296	.0258	.0449	.0371

Legends: Y: 1962 Occupational Status
          W: First Job Status
          U: Education
          X: Father's Occupational Status
          V: Father's Education

a. Deviation index is given by: $d_i = \sqrt{\sum_j (M_i - S_{ij})^2 / 10}$

Where i refers to the bivariate relationships indicated in column one; M_i refers to the underlying value from the Blau-Duncan Model; S_{ij} refers to the corresponding sample estimate where j stands for 10 different samplings.

b. Overall Deviation Index = $\sqrt{\sum_i \sum_j (M_i - S_{ij})^2 / 100}$

Source of the model: (Blau- and Duncan, 1967: 169.)

In contrast to Haitovsky's findings, our simulations indicate that the pairwise deletion performs better than listwise deletion, at least for the present model. Pairwise deletion produces less mean deviation from the model with respect to not only the whole matrix but also every individual coefficient but one (the exception is underlined in Table 1). The result is about the same whether we consider the sample correlation matrices or covariance matrices. To evaluate the fit between

TABLE 2
**Sampling Variability as Measured by the Mean Deviation
of Sample Coefficients from Population Values,
When There is No Missing Data**[a]

Bivariate Relation	Mean Deviation from the Model	
	Correlations	Covariances
YW	.0216	.0333
YU	.0163	.0350
YX	.0219	.0320
YU	.0238	.0295
WU	.0194	.0348
WX	.0201	.0293
WV	.0258	.0398
UX	.0285	.0423
UV	.0236	.0391
XV	.0283	.0462
Overall	.0232	.0361

a. Based on the same samples as presented in Table 1, except that coefficients are calculated before some information is made randomly missing.

the model and the sample covariance matrix, one may also include variance terms in the calculation of the index. Since such an inclusion produces similar results, we have not included them in Table 1.

The deviation indices in Table 1 alone do not provide full information about the effects of employing these two methods of handling missing data. We also need the sampling variability of the same size samples with no missing data. Table 2 contains information from samples without missing data. Sample correlations and covariances from samples without missing data deviate from the model to almost the same extent as the sample coefficients based on pairwise deletions Compare, for instance, .0258 from the third column of Table 1, to .0232 from Table 2. In other words, most of the variability observed

TABLE 3
Simulation Results Using the Blau-Duncan Correlation Matrix: 10 Samples of 1000 Cases Each from a Multivariate Normal Population Where 10% of the Cases are Missing Randomly From Each Variable: Unstandardized Path Coefficients[a]

Path Coefficient		Mean Deviation from the Model	
		Listwise Deletion	Pairwise Deletion
YW	.2881	.0271	.0308
YU	.3983	.0348	.0270
·YX	.1205	.0298	.0282
YV	-.0139	.0378	.0277
WU	.4326	.0333	.0256
WX	.2144	.0440	.0398
WV	.0254	.0467	.0416
UX	.2784	.0364	.0351
UV	.3094	.0393	.0369
XV	.5160	.0365	.0315
Overall Index		.0370	.0328

Where Y is regressed on W, U X and U; W is regressed U,X and V; U is regressed on X and V; X on V for convenience.

a. See Table 1 for source and legends for the variables.

in Table 1 is due to the general sampling variability and not to the problem of missing data.

Since Haitovsky's findings were based on the examination of the unstandardized regression coefficients, we thought it prudent to examine such regression coefficients as well. In Table 3, we present results based on the direct examination of regression coefficients, representing the values of the presumed population model. Then the sample path coefficients (unstandardized)[8] are compared to these

TABLE 4
Mean Deviations of Sample Covariances
from Population covariances for 10 Samples
of 1000 Cases, Each Based on the Blau-Duncan
Correlation Matrix by Percent Randomly Missing[a]

% of Missing from each Variable	1% Missing	2% Missing	5% Missing	10% Missing
Listwise	.0383	.0394	.0426	.0449
Pairwise	.0363	.0376	.0378	.0371

a. See Table 1 for source of data and description of deviation indexes.

underlying values. The conclusion is the same; pairwise deletion still fares better than listwise deletion.

In order to check whether our findings are due to the excessive amount of missing data, we repeated the simulations while decreasing the proportion of missing observations on each variable. Note that listwise deletion would retain only about 590 cases while pairwise deletion will retain about 810 cases when 10% of the cases are randomly missing on each variable. As shown in Table 4, however, pairwise deletion maintains its superiority as the proportion of missing values on a variable is decreased to about 1%.

The sample size differences between a pairwise deletion and a listwise deletion is greatly affected by the number of variables involved. With 10% missing on each variable (randomly), listwise deletion with a five-variable data set would lose about 410 cases out of 1000, but would lose only 270 cases with a three-variable data set. In contrast, pairwise deletion would retain a data base of 810 cases regardless of the number of variables involved. Table 5 illustrates the effects of such changes in the data base as we decrease the number of variables. As expected from the result of Table 4, pairwise deletion performs better.

Although we cannot generalize our finding because it is based on a fixed (large) sample size (1000 cases) and a fixed (moderate) correlation matrix, it is clear that the use of pairwise deletion can be better than the use of listwise deletion for a certain type of data and that it is premature to preclude the issue on the basis of Haitovsky's simulations.[9] For survey researchers with a relatively large data set, where the strengths of the bivariate associations are moderate, pairwise

TABLE 5
Overall Mean Deviation of Sample Covariances, when the Number of Variables Are Reduced (10% missing from each variable.)[a]

	2 Variables	3 Variables	4 Variables	5 Variables
Listwise Deletion	.0376[b]	.0433	.0393	.0453
Pairwise Deletion	.0376[c]	.0373	.0370	.0375

a. See Table 1 for source of data and description of deviation indexes.
b. The variables used in these simulations are: Y and U; Y, U, and W; Y, X, U, W; and all five.
c. The two methods are equivalent.

deletion should remain a viable option provided the observations are missing randomly. But if one is interested in retaining as many cases as possible as in index construction, the use of pairwise deletion in the stage of parameter estimation (such as factor loadings) will not be of much help. One must find ways of removing missing values before constructing a composite index, otherwise the data loss will be as severe as in the case of listwise deletion.

ESTIMATING MISSING VALUES

There are three main reasons why a researcher might consider replacing missing information with some estimate: (1) to simplify calculation of statistics, (2) to improve parameter estimations, or (3) to retain as many cases as possible in constructing scales out of many variables.

The first reason has become trivial as researchers rely increasingly on computers for their calculations. But there are situations in which ease of presentation and/or interpretation may justify using such a method even with a computer (Draper and Stoneman, 1964). An example in point has already been given in the section on the use of dummy indicator variables; when the mean values are used in the place of the missing values of X, the partial regression coefficients for the indicator variables X_a and X' (with mean replaced for missing values) become equivalent to simple regression coefficients. Of course, it also implies that a simple regression of Y on X' will be equivalent to a regression based on the m cases only. (Wilks, 1932; also see Afifi and Elashof, 1966; Cohen and Cohen, 1975.) But this does not mean that the correlation between the two for the m cases will be the same because the variance of X′ will be less than the variance of X for the first m cases.[10]

Another example is found when the orthogonality of an experimental design is destroyed by the existence of some missing data and the use of neutral values can simplify the calculation and presentation of the result (Cochran and Cox, 1957).

MAXIMUM UTILIZATION OF INFORMATION

Reexamination of the pattern A (below) will reveal that neither listwise deletion nor pairwise deletion uses all the available information. For the estimation of a covariance, both procedures use the same data base and therefore are equivalent in this case. If there is some relationship between Y and X,

$$X: x_1, x_2, \ldots x_m \ldots x_N$$
$$Y: y_1, y_2, \ldots y_m$$

(Pattern A)

and missing values are independent of the values of Y given the values of X—therefore, the observed covariation between Y and X is unaffected in the long run by the existence of missing values in Y—then the X values for the last $(N - m)$ cases contain some information about the possible values of the missing Ys.[11]

Estimates based on the utilization of all the available data are given by (Wilks, 1932; Anderson, 1957).

$$m_x = \Sigma X_i / N \quad (i = 1, 2, \ldots N)$$
$$m_y = m_y^* + b_{yx} (m_x - m_x^*)$$
$$V_x = \Sigma (X_i - m_m)^2 / N \quad (i = 1, 2, \ldots N)$$
$$V_y = b_{yx} V_x + V_{y \cdot x}$$
$$V_{yx} = b_{yx} V_x$$

where
$$m_y^* = \Sigma Y_i / m \quad (i = 1\ 2, \ldots m)$$
$$m_x^* = \Sigma X_i / m \quad (i = 1\ 2, \ldots m)$$
$$b_{yx} = \Sigma \left\{ (X_i - m_x^*)(Y_i - M_y^*) \right\} / \Sigma (X_i - m_x)^2 \quad (i = 1, 2, \ldots m)$$
$$V_{y \cdot x} = \Sigma (Y_i - m_y^*) / m - b_{yx} V_x$$

In other words, estimates of the mean and variance of Y can be improved if information on X and the relationships between Y and X are utilized. The solutions above are derived using the least-squares principle, but they will be maximum-likelihood solutions if the underlying population distribution is bivariate normal and these estimates are in general more efficient than estimates based on only the first m cases (e.g., Wilks, 1932; Anderson, 1957).

It must be noted that if there is no underlying association between Y and X, no information would be gained by following this type of strategy and as the association between the two variables gets stronger the greater will be the gain in efficiency (see Little, 1976b).

In arriving at the more efficient estimates of parameters, the values of missing Ys are not actually replaced by the estimated values. Such estimation of parameters is possible only because the missing data pattern A is extremely simple. We turn now to a more complex pattern of missing data.

ESTIMATION OF MISSING VALUES AND ITERATIVE SOLUTIONS

Consider now two relatively more complex missing data patterns, B and C. In pattern B:

$$X: x_1, x_2, \ldots x_m, y_{m+1}, \ldots x_{m+n}, *, \ldots * \qquad , **$$
$$\text{(Pattern B)}$$
$$Y: y_1, y_2, \ldots y_m, * \qquad , \ldots * \qquad , y_{m+n}, \ldots y_{N=m+n+w}, **$$

(* represents missing data)

missing values are present on both X and Y. We would normally delete the cases with no valid information and consider only the first N cases. In pattern C, we present only abbreviated data:

Types:	1	2	3	4	5	6	7	8	
X:	/	/	/	*	/	*	*	*	(Pattern C)
Y:	/	/	*	/	*	/	*	*	
Z:	/	*	/	/	*	*	/	*	

(/ indicates nonmissing data; * indicates missing data)

There are 2^p (where p = number of variables and $2^3 = 8$) types of data. Out of these potential types only the last one does not contain any information. Therefore, we would normally consider only the first (8 – 1) types, deleting the last type out of analysis. In particular note that type 7 would have been deleted in bivariate context, and that in general, the greater the number of variables under consideration (provided they are all associated with each other to some extent), the greater the utilization of existing information.

Returning to pattern B, and extending the strategies used in dealing with the A data, we may try to estimate underlying parameters from the examination of the two different combinations of data. (1) Use the first (m + n) cases to retrieve the lost information due to n missing values on Y, and (2) use (m + w) cases to retrieve the lost information due to missing values on X. But the resulting estimates are likely to disagree. A general solution to deal with situations like B, as well as C, is as follows (Beale and Little, 1974):

(1) Use available information to estimate missing values;

(2) after replacing the missing values with estimated values, estimate the parameters from the data containing estimated values (with proper adjustment);

(3) reestimate the missing values, using the estimated parameters given in step (2);

(4) repeat the process (1) through (3) until the estimated values converge.

More specifically, the steps are:

(1) Estimate regression coefficients for each type of missing data, while using all the available information. Then insert the predicted values based on the regression in the place of missing data (for convenience, one can use the covariance matrix based on listwise deletion for the initial estimation of missing values).

(2) Then estimate the parameters—mean (m_j), variance, and covariance (v_{jk})—by:

$$m_j = \Sigma X_{ij} / N$$
$$V_{jk} = \Sigma \left\{ (X_{ij} - m_j)(X_{ik} - m_k) + V_{jk \cdot P_i} \right\} / N, \quad (i = 1, 2, \ldots N)$$

where $v_{jk \cdot P_i}$ refers to the partial covariance between variable j and k while P_i represents the other variables in the set with valid information on case i—(X_{ij} is the observed value if not missing).

(3) Repeat the process until convergence. The only aspect requiring comment is the adjustment term $V_{jk \cdot P_i}$ in step (2). This is the term that

vanishes unless information is missing on both variables j and k (which implies, of course, in calculating variance $[v_{jj}]$ the term must appear whenever information is missing on one variable). This adjustment term is necessary because the estimated values reduce the variance of a variable and reduce or increase the covariance depending upon the direction of partial relationship between j and k (see, e.g., Buck, 1960; Beale and Little, 1974).

For the demonstration that such a solution leads to the maximum likelihood solution proposed by Orchard and Woodbury (1972) when multivariate normality is assumed and that this iterated solution is in general superior to other methods, Beale and Little (1974) should be consulted. Among the methods Beale and Little (1974) examine are (1) ordinary regression solutions based on listwise deletion and (2) the method of using regression estimates of missing values by Buck (1960). Unfortunately, they did not consider the regression solution based on pairwise deletion, relying partly on the evidence presented by Haitovsky (1968). On the basis of our simulation presented earlier, we must consider for now that the relative merits of pairwise deletion and the iterative solution are unknown for a large sample with moderate correlations.[12]

ESTIMATION OF MISSING VALUES WITHOUT ITERATION

For those who have no access to custom computer programming, we will mention a few other procedures of estimating missing values and parameters:

(1) Assigning regression estimates to missing values and estimating parameters with some adjustments (Buck, 1960);

(2) assigning regression estimates and random component with equal-expected variance as the residual variance $(v_{yx \cdot Pi})$, then estimating parameters using ordinary regression routines;

(3) estimating the missing values by using principal component transformation, then estimating parameters (by Dear, cited in Afifi and Elashof, 1966; and Timm, 1970).

The first procedure above is to use regression estimates as one would do in the first step of iterative solution but without iterations.

The accuracy of the first estimate is more critical in this method than in the iterative solution. Therefore, one may not use the matrix based on listwise deletion but should use a different matrix for every type of missing value pattern. This method was found to be generally superior to assigning means to missing values or to Dear's method, but not in every case (see Timm, 1970). One point needing special attention is that variances and covariances calculated from the variables (with estimated values replacing the missing values) have to be corrected for bias (as was the case in iterative solutions).

The second procedure is a modification of Buck's. Instead of replacing the missing values with regression estimates, this method replaces them with regression estimates plus a random component in order to simulate the degree of residual variance existing in the data:

Value to use in
the place of the $\qquad = \hat{X}_{ij} +$ (error of estimate) (random normal number)
missing value on X_{ij}

Because the random component reintroduces the expected residual variation in the predicted data, one can use ordinary regression algorithms to estimate various parameters. That is, it obviates the need for adjustment in the estimation of parameters. At least one popular statistical package, SPSS (Nie et al., 1975), allows the generation of random numbers to be used in such situations along with the variables under consideration.

The third procedure applies principal-components analysis to the correlation matrix based on listwise deletion. The principal components for the missing values are then estimated from the existing data, using the weights given by the principal-components analysis. Next, the principal components are transformed back to raw data. Then the raw data (with the estimated values included) are used for parameter estimation (see Afifi and Elashoff, 1966; and Timm, 1970). Timm's (1970) simulations do support this solution as preferable to Buck's only when the number of variables is relatively large in relation to the sample size, correlations are not moderate, and the missing information is substantial. Overall, however, he finds that this procedure is inferior to Buck's.

Finally, although all the procedures for estimating missing values involve considerably more complex computations, they have one

TABLE 6

**Overall Comparison of Various Methods, Using the
Blau-Duncan Matrix as Model: 10 Samples of 1000 Cases,
10% Missing on Each Variable**

Method	Mean Deviations from the Model				
	(1)	(2)	(3)	(4)	(5)
Correlation Matrix	.0497	.0296	.0258	.0286	.0232
Covariance Matrix	.0891	.0449	.0371	.0388	.0361

Legends:
(1) Means assigned to missing values
(2) Listwise deletion of missing data
(3) Pairwise deletion of missing data
(4) Regression estimate and random component in the place of missing values
(5) Complete Sample

definite advantage over simple solutions such as pairwise and listwise deletion: in constructing scales out of many variables, the estimated values can be used in the place of missing values. Furthermore, the estimated values are based on a more refined use of the available information than simply replacing missing values with the mean as is found as an option in at least one packaged program for scale construction (Nie et al., 1975).

To recapitulate some salient points from various computer simulations, Buck (1960) and Haitovsky (1968) find listwise deletion preferable to pairwise deletion. Timm (1970) finds that Buck's (1960) regression solution is superior in general to the regression solution based on listwise deletion; Beale and Little (1974) find the iterative maximum likelihood solution superior to Buck's regression solution; assigning means to missing values does not fare well in comparison with any of the other solutions mentioned above and Dear's principal components solution appears to lag behind Buck's regression solution. Against this background, we find that for a large data set with moderate correlations, the pairwise deletion performs better than the listwise deletion. It is obvious that we need additional studies comparing these various methods using sociological data.

Some preliminary results from our own simulations are presented in Table 6.[13] Most of the data presented in Table 6 are from earlier tables. The only new information is the performance of the regression method with a random component compared with other standard procedures. We find that replacing missing values by this method does not do as well as pairwise deletion but is superior to listwise deletion. More importantly, parameter estimates based on pairwise deletion and the regression-random component method are fairly close in their efficiency to the estimates based on the complete samples with no missing data.

CONCLUSION

We have tried to abstain from making general assertions as to the superiority of one method over another because convenience and feasibility must also be considered in making the final decision. Furthermore, when the sample size is very large (say 1000 or more), the choice may not make very much difference (Beale and Little, 1974). It is our hope that the preceding discussion alerts survey researchers to possible complications arising from missing data and to the fact that they may be using less than an optimal solution to the problem.

Since we have confined our discussion largely to the multivariate case where variables are measured on at least an interval scale and are considered to be random variables, a few words are in order concerning other situations not covered in this paper.

First, in least-squares regression and analysis of variance, it is customary to consider the independent variables as fixed constants. When one deals with survey data, however, there is no compelling reason to consider the independent variables as fixed constants other than the fact that such an assumption (although not very realistic) can simplify the derivation of the sampling distributions of parameter estimates (Johnston, 1972). On the other hand, if one has a data set with genuinely fixed independent variables as in an experimental design, the researcher should consult specialized sources (e.g., Hartley and Hocking, 1971).

For situations in which some variables are categorical, see Hartley and Hocking (1971), Jackson (1969), and Chan and Dunn (1974).

See also Hertel (1976) and the report of the U.S. Bureau of the Census for a description of the "hot-deck" procedure which is especially suited for large data sets such as the national census. Either because of their reviews of the literature or their generality of scope, the following sources are especially valuable: Afifi and Elashoff, (1966, 1967, 1969); Hartley and Hocking (1971); Orchard and Woodbury (1972); Beale and Little (1974); Cohen and Cohen (1975); and Rubin (1976). Orchard and Woodbury (1972) contains a classified bibliography. See also Press and Scott (1974; 1976) for an introduction to the growing literature on the Bayesian approach. A few recent materials dealing with specialized topics are included in the bibliography without comment.

NOTES

1. Computer packages, such as SPSS (Nie et al., 1975), have made it easy for a researcher to choose either a *listwise* deletion or a *pairwise* deletion of missing data by making them standard options in various multivariate analysis. A *pairwise* deletion estimates bivariate relationships on the basis of cases for which information is complete for the two variables only, and then constructs a synthetic multivariate data matrix from the bivariate matrix.

2. When the correlation or covariance matrix is not consistent, one may get regression results in which the multiple correlation is greater than one or less than zero. The statistical results from such a matrix would be meaningless (see Cohen and Cohen) for an illustration of the problem, 1975).

3. In this case, the existence of missing data on the variable of interest, voting, is due simply to the fact that the respondent was too young to vote. We may thus view the legal-age restriction on voting as essentially unrelated to the respondent's overall propensity for political participation. Yet, at the same time, a prime research objective may be to construct a general index of political participation such that complete information on voting behavior is necessary.

4. We do not examine all the possible patterns of missing data because, in most instances, the expected frequencies for some of the categories such as $(M_1 M_2 M_3)$, will be too small to be used for x^2 testing. For the same reason, variables with too small a number of cases, producing M less than 5 cases, may be dropped from the test.

5. One may further refine x^2 tests by introducing Yate's correction for continuity if the expected frequencies are relatively small (Cramer, 1946: 445), or may use Fisher's exact test.

6. See note 2 above.

7. For the generation of random numbers see Newman and Odel (1971), and for the generation of population correlation matrices see Kaiser and Dickman (1962). We

have generated random-normal numbers using the "Super-Duper" program (from Duke University). After creating samples with a given population correlation matrix according to Kaiser and Dickman's method, we augmented the data set with an equal number of variables using the random-uniform number generator provided by SPSS. The proportion of cases made "missing" on a given variable was determined by the range of the associated random-uniform variable. For this reason, the proportion of missing observations is not fixed but fluctuates slightly from sample to sample.

8. We assume the basic model in the population to be multivariate normal with mean = 0, and variance = 1. However, samples from such a population would not necessarily have a mean of 0, and a variance of 1. Therefore, the sample variance and covariance would be different, although they should be equivalent in our population model.

9. We hope to report on further comparisons of these two options as well as other procedures which we are currently investigating with the support of NIMH Grant #30407-01.

10. Hertel (1976) illustrates this point and advocates the replacement of regression estimates instead of the mean for the missing values. But regression estimates also introduce biases into the calculation of variances and covariances. These points are discussed in a later section of the text.

11. Cases (1) and (2) of the missing data patterns would qualify. On the other hand, if the missing data are produced by the process described in (5), an attempt to retrieve information would be erroneous. Other patterns, such as (3) and (4), would allow one to retrieve some information from the available data but would not allow unbiased estimation (see Little, 1976b; Rubin, 1976).

12. This and other problems of missing data are now under investigation (NIMH Grant #30407-01); we will report the result in the near future.

13. Due to special programming chores required to evaluate Buck's regression method and the iterative method, we do not yet have results comparing the two methods but we hope to report them soon (see note 12).

REFERENCES

AFIFI, A. A. and R. M. ELASHOFF (1969) "Missing observations in multivariate statistics IV: a note on simple linear regression." Amer. Statistical Association 64 (March): 359-365.

——— (1969) "Missing observations in multivariate statistics III: large sample analysis of simple linear regression." Amer. Statistical Association 64 (March): 337-358.

——— (1967) "Missing observations in multivariate statistics II. Point estimation in simple linear regression." Amer. Statistical Association 62 (March): 10-29.

——— (1966) "Missing observations in multivariate statistics I. Review of the literature." Amer. Statistical Association 61: 595-604.

ANDERSON, T. W. (1957) "Maximum likelihood estimates for a multivariate normal distribution when some observations are missing." Amer. Statistical Association 52: 200-203.

BEALE, E. M. and R.J.A. LITTLE (1974) "Missing values in multivariate analysis." J. of the Royal Statistical Society, London 37.

BLAU, P. M. and O. D. DUNCAN (1967) The American Occupational Structure. New York: John Wiley.

BLOOMFIELD, P. (1970) "Spectral analysis with randomly missing observations." Royal Statistical Society, London B, 32: 369-380.

BOX, M. J., N. R. DRAPER, and W. G. HUNTER (1970) "Missing values in multi-response non-linear model fitting." Technometrics, 12 (August): 613-320.

BUCK, S. F. (1960) "A method of estimation of missing values in multivariate data suitable for use with an electronic computer." Royal Statistical Society, London B, 22: 302-306.

CHAN, L. S. and O. J. DUNN (1974) "A note on the asymptotic aspect of the treatment of missing values in discriminant analysis." J. of the Amer. Statistical Association 69 (September): 672-673.

CHOW, G. C. and AN-LOH LIN (1976) "Best linear unbiased estimation of missing observations in an economic time series." J. of the Amer. Statistical Association 71 (September): 719-721.

COCHRAN, W. G. and G. M. COX (1957) Experimental Designs. New York: John Wiley.

COHEN, J. and P. COHEN (1975) Applied Multiple Regression/Correlation Analysis. New York: Erlbaum.

CRAMER, H. (1946) Mathematical Methods of Statistics. Princeton: Princeton Univ. Press.

DAGENAIS, M. G. (1974) "Multiple regression analysis with incomplete observations, from a Bayesian viewpoint." Stud. in Bayesian Econometrics and Statistics.

——— (1971) "Utilization of incomplete observations in regression analysis." J. of the Amer. Statistical Association 66 (March): 93-98.

DRAPER, N. R. and D. M. STONEMAN (1964) "Estimating missing values in unreplicated two-level factorial and fractional factorial designs." Biometrics 20 (September): 443-458.

GLASSER, M. (1964) "Linear regression analysis with missing observations among the independent variables." J. of the Amer. Statistical Association 59: 834-844.

GOODMAN, L. A. (1968) "The analysis of cross-classified data: independence, quasi-independence and interactions in contingency tables with or without missing entries." J. of the Amer. Statistical Association, 63 (December): 1091-1131.

FIENBERG, S. E. (1970) "Quasi-independence and maximum likelihood estimation in incomplete contingency tables." J. of the Amer. Statistical Association 65 (December): 1610-1616.

HAITOVSKY, Y. (1968) "Missing data in regression analysis." Royal Statistical Society. London, B, 30: 67-82.

HARTLEY, H. O. and R.R. HOCKING (1971) "The analysis of incomplete data," Biometrics, 27 (December): 783-823.

HARTWELL, T. D. and D. W. GAYLOR (1973) "Estimating variance components for two-way disproportionate data with missing cells by method of unweighted means." J. of the Amer. Statistical Association 68 (June): 379-383.

HERTEL, B. R. (1976) "Minimizing error variance introduced by missing data routines in survey analysis." Soc. Methods and Research 4 (May): 459-474.

HOCKING, R. R. and H. H. OXSPRING (1971) "Maximum likelihood estimation with incomplete observations in regression analysis." J. of the Amer. Statistical Association 66 (March): 65-70.

HOCKING, R. R. and W. B. SMITH (1968) "Estimation of parameters in the multivariate normal distribution with missing observations." J. of the Amer. Statistical Association 63 (March): 159-173.

JACKSON, E. C. (1968) "Missing values in linear multiple discriminant analysis." Biometrics 24 (December): 835-844.

JOHNSTON, J. (1972) Econometric Methods. New York: McGraw-Hill.

KAISER, H. F. and K. DICKMAN (1962) "Sample and population score matrices and sample correlation matrices from an arbitrary population correlation matrix." Psychometrika 27: 179-182.

KELEJIAN, H. H. (1969) "Missing observations in multivariate regression: efficiency of a first-order method." Amer. Statistical Association 64 1609-1616.

KIM, JAE-ON, N. H. NIE, and S. VERBA, (1977) "A note on factor analyzing dichotomous variables: the case of political participation." Pol. Methodology (Spring): 39-62.

LIN, PI-ERH (1973) "Procedures for testing the difference of means with incomplete data." J. of the Amer. Statistical Association 68 (September): 699-703.

——— (1971) "Estimation procedures for difference of means with missing data." J. of the Amer. Statistical Association 66 (September): 634-636.

——— and L. E. STIVERS (1975) "Testing for equality of means with incomplete data on one variable: a Monte Carlo study." J. of the Amer. Soc. Association 70 (March): 190-193.

LITTLE, R.J.A. (1976a) "Comments on paper by D. B. Rubin." Biometrika 63, 3: 590-591.

——— (1976b) "Inference about means from incomplete multivariate data." Biometrika 63: 593-604.

McDONALD, L.(1971) "On the estimation of missing data in the multivariate linear model." Biometrics 27 (September): 535-543.

MEHTA, J. S. and P.A.V.B. SWAMY (1973) "Bayesian analysis of a bivariate normal distribution with incomplete observations." J. of the Amer. Soc. Association 68 (December): 922-927.

MORRISON, D. F. (1971) "Expectations and variances of maximum likelihood estimates of multivariate normal distribution parameters with missing data." J. of the Amer. Soc. Association 66 (September): 602-604.

NEWMAN, T. G. and P. L. ODELL (1971) The Generation of Random Variates. New York: Hafner Publishing.

NIE, N. H., C. H. HULL, J. G. JENKINS, K. STEINBRENNER, and D. H. BENT (1975) Statistical Package for the Social Sciences. New York: McGraw-Hill.

ORCHARD, T. and M. A. WOODBURY (1972) "A missing information principle: theory and applications." Proceedings of the sixth Berkeley Symposium on Mathematical Statistics and Probability, Theory of Statistics, Univ. of California Press.

PRESS, S. J. and A. J. SCOTT (1976) "Missing variables in Bayesian regression, II." J. of the Amer. Soc. Association 71 (June): 366-369.

——— (1974) "Missing variables in Bayesian regression." Studies in Bayesian Econometrics and Statistics. Amsterdam: North Holland: 259-272.

RUBIN, D. B. (1976) "Comparing regressions when some predictor values are missing." Technometrics 23 (May): 201-205.

——— (1976) "Inference and missing data." Biometrika 63, 3: 581-592.

———(1974) "Characterizing the estimation of parameters in incomplete-data problems." J. of the Amer. Statistical Association 69, 346: 467-474.

TIMM, N. H. (1970) "The estimation of variance-covariance and correlation matrices from incomplete data." Psychometrika 35 (December): 417-437.

U.S. Bureau of the Census (1970) 1970 Census User's Guide. 1: 26-28.

WILKS, S. S. (1932) "Moments and distributions of population parameters from fragmentary samples." Annals of Mathematical Statistics 3 (August), 163-195.

WOODBURY, M. A. (1971) "Discussion of paper by Hartley and Hocking." Biometrics 27 (December): 808-823.

Jae-On Kim is Associate Professor of Sociology at the University of Iowa. His areas of interest are political sociology, social stratification, and quantitative methodology.

James Curry is a Ph.D. candidate in Sociology at the University of Iowa. He is interested in social stratification and quantitative methodology.

Biases due to measurement errors in an earnings function for nonblack males are assessed by estimating unobserved variable models with data from the Income Supplement Reinterview program of the March 1973 Current Population Survey and from the remeasurement program of the 1973 Occupational Changes in a Generation-II survey. We find that reports of social origins, educational and occupational attainments, labor supply, and earnings of nonblack males are subject to primarily random response errors. Logarithmic earnings is one of the most accurately measured indicators of socioeconomic success. Further, retrospective reports of status variables are as reliable as contemporaneous reports. When measurement errors are ignored for nonblacks, the total economic return to schooling is underestimated by about 16% and the effects of some background variables are underestimated by as much as 15%. The total effects of first and current job status are underestimated by about 20% when measurement errors are ignored, as are the unmediated effects of current job status. Conflicting evidence is presented on whether respondents tend to understate the consistency between their earnings and educational attainments in the Current Population Survey. If there is such a tendency, unmediated effects of education are modestly understated when response errors are ignored, and they are overstated if no such tendency exists.

RESPONSE ERROR IN EARNINGS FUNCTIONS
FOR NONBLACK MALES

WILLIAM T. BIELBY
University of California-Santa Barbara

ROBERT M. HAUSER
University of Wisconsin-Madison

Structural equation models of the social and economic determinants of earnings have been used by social scientists of

AUTHORS' NOTE: *This research was supported by NSF Grants GI-31604 and GI-44336, NICHD Grant HD-05876, NIGMS Grant GM-01526, and by institutional support from the College of Agricultural and Life Services. We have worked closely with David L. Featherman in the design, collection, and management of the data on which this analysis is based. Any opinions, findings, conclusions, or recommendations are those of the authors and do not necessarily reflect the views of the National Science Foundation or other supporting agencies.*

diverse perspectives. Sociologists have specified earnings functions as part of status-attainment models in order to examine the relative impact of schooling and social origins on socioeconomic success (Duncan et al., 1972; Jencks, et al., 1972; Alexander, et al., 1975; Sewell and Hauser, 1975; Hauser and Daymont, 1977). Similar functions have been used by economists to construct human-capital models of the generation of income inequality (Mincer, 1974; Blinder, 1976; Rosenzweig, 1976). Marxist sociologists and economists, while taking issue with the substantive foundations of status attainment and human-capital models, have also employed structural-equation models of the determinants of earnings in their empirical representations of the generation of income inequality (Bowles, 1972; Bowles and Gintis, 1976; Wright and Perrone, 1977). Thus, while disagreements continue over conceptualization, the magnitudes of structural coefficients, and the appropriate specification of structural models, there exists remarkable consensus that a structural-equation model is an appropriate empirical representation of the determinants of economic success.

It is also generally agreed that response errors (as well as the omission of ability or other common causes of schooling and of socioeconomic achievement) may bias estimates of the socioeconomic returns to schooling and social origins. However, the size and the importance of such biases have been points of controversy. Jencks et al., drawing on the work of Siegel and Hodge (1968), conclude that "random measurement error is of relatively little importance in research of the kind described here" (1972:336). Bowles (1972:S222) asserts that "social class background is considerably more important as a determinant of both educational attainment and economic success than has been indicated in recent analogous statistical treatments by Duncan and others." Bowles argues that retrospective reports of parental statuses are much less reliable than respondents' reports of their own attainments and that the effects of origin variables are consequently underestimated. Unfortunately, attempts to assess biases due to response errors have been flawed by a lack of appropriate data, by inadequate specifications, and by crude estimation procedures (see Bielby, 1976: 11-61, and Bielby et al., 1977a for a more detailed discussion of these issues).

In order to help resolve the controversy surrounding response bias in models of socioeconomic success, a carefully designed remeasurement program was included as part of the 1973 Occupational Changes in a

Generation study. Recently developed statistical procedures that allow for unobservable variables in structural-equation models (Jöreskog, 1970; 1973) were applied to these data and to data from the March 1973 Current Population Survey income-reinterview program in order to assess the extent of response error in measures of socioeconomic variables and to assess the biases in structural coefficients resulting from those errors. Our findings for a model of occupational attainment have been reported elsewhere. For nonblack males, we found compelling evidence that response errors in reports of social origins, education, and occupational attainments are mutually uncorrelated, and we found that retrospective reports of social origins are reported about as accurately as more recent attainments (Bielby, 1976; Bielby et al., 1977a; 1977b).[1]

The research reported here extends our earlier findings to include the determinants of earnings among nonblack males. Unless the errors in reports of earnings are correlated with errors in reports of other variables, our findings should be similar to those summarized above (since we already know the relative quality of most predetermined variables in the earnings equation). Furthermore, since earned income does not appear as a predetermined variable in any of our models, random measurement error in reports of earnings cannot bias metric structural coefficients; it can only cause an overestimate of residual variance and uniform underestimates of standardized structural coefficients in the earnings equation.

1973 OCG AND CPS DATA

The 1973 OCG (Occupational Changes in a Generation) study was designed to replicate the 1962 OCG study conducted by Blau and Duncan (1967). The replicate study, executed in conjunction with the Current Population Survey (CPS), represents approximately 53 million males in the civilian noninstitutional population between the ages of 20 and 65 in March 1973. Data from the 1973 study allow us to estimate and test a variety of models of response error and to assess the effects of plausible error structures on parameters of the achievement process.

The data were collected in four surveys during 1973. First, educational and labor-force data were obtained from the March 1973 CPS household interviews; in about three-fourths of the cases the CPS respondent was the spouse of the designated male. Second, a subsample of households containing about 1000 CPS male respondents was select-ed for inclusion in the March CPS Income Supplement Reinterview (ISR) survey. Beginning about one week after completion of the CPS interview, personal (and in some cases, telephone) interviews were con-ducted with respondents in these households to obtain a second report of selected CPS labor-force and income items. Third, the CPS data were supplemented in the fall of 1973 with social background and occupational-career data from the mail-out, mail-back OCG question-naire (OCGQ); in about three-fourths of the cases the OCGQ respon-dent was the designated male. Responses to OCGQ were obtained from this questionnaire or subsequent telephone or personal follow-ups for more than 27,000 members of the experienced civilian labor force; the overall response rate was greater than 88%. Fourth, a random sub-sample of about 1000 OCGQ respondents (600 nonblacks and 400 blacks) was selected for inclusion in the OCG remeasurement (OCGR) survey. Approximately three weeks after the mail return of their OCG questionnaires, telephone (and in a few cases, personal) interviews were conducted with these respondents to obtain a second report of selected items on the OCG questionnaire.

Table 1 shows which variables were measured on each of the four occasions: CPS, ISR, OCGQ, and OCGR. Educational attainment (x_{41}), current (March) occupation (x_{61}), weeks worked in 1972 (x_{71}), earned income in 1972 (x_{81}), and whether the sample person usually worked full- or part-time in 1972 ($x_{11,1}$) were ascertained in the March CPS interview. A second report of weeks worked (x_{72}) and earned in-come (x_{82}) were obtained from the income-supplement reinterview. Reports of the three social background variables, father's (or other head of household's) occupation (x_{13}) and educational attainment (x_{23}) and parental family income (x_{33}), were obtained from the fall OCG ques-tionnaire. Also, the fall questionnaire ascertained the man's first full-time civilian job after completing schooling (x_{53}) and a second report of his educational attainment (x_{43}). (The second measurement of ED (education) was not intended to supplant the CPS item, but rather to improve the respondent's recall of the timing of schooling and labor force entry.) Also obtained from the fall OCG questionnaire were a measure of labor-force experience (x_{93}, $x_{10,3}$), and whether or not the sample person belonged to a labor union ($x_{12,3}$). Within the OCGR sub-sample, each of the social background variables (x_{14}, x_{24}, x_{34}), education (x_{44}), and first job (x_{54}) was measured again. We were not able to ascer-

TABLE 1
Timing of Measurements in the 1973 CPS and OCG Surveys

Variable	March 1973 CPS household interview (CPS)	Spring 1973 supplement reinterview (ISR)	Fall 1973 OCG Questionnaire (OCGQ)	Fall 1973 OCG remeasurement interview (OCGR)
1. Father's occupational status (FO)	--	--	x_{13}	x_{14}
2. Father's educational attainment (FE)	--	--	x_{23}	x_{24}
3. Parental income (PI)	--	--	x_{33}	x_{34}
4. Educational attainment (ED)	x_{41}	--	x_{43}	x_{44}
5. Occupational status of first job after completing schooling (O1)	--	--	x_{53}	x_{54}
6. Current occupational status (March or Fall) (OC)	x_{61}	--	--	x_{64}
7. Weeks worked in 1972 (WKS)	x_{71}	x_{72}	--	--
8. Earned income in 1972 (LNEARN)	x_{81}	x_{82}	--	--
9. Experience (years since began first job after completing schooling)(EX)	--	--	x_{93}	--
10. (Experience $- 20)^2/10$ (EX2)	--	--	$x_{10,3}$	--
11. Working full-time (FT)	$x_{11,1}$	--	--	--
12. Labor union membership (UN)	--	--	$x_{12,3}$	--

tain March 1973 occupation in the OCGR interviews, and instead a report of current (Fall 1973) occupation (x_{64}) was obtained. While some job mobility occurred between the spring and fall surveys, we disregard it here on the argument that occupational status changes were negligible over the six or seven-month period. Consequently, our estimates of unreliability in the reporting of current occupational status include effects of short-term job mobility as well as response error.

In summary, we have: (1) two measures of education and one measure of each other variable for the full CPS-OCGQ sample; (2) two measures each of education, earnings, and weeks worked and one measure of each other variable for the ISR subsample; and (3) three measures of education, two measures of each indicator of social origins, two measures each of first and current job status, and one measure of each of the remaining variables for the OCGR subsample.

Each of the occupation reports was scaled using Duncan SEI scores for detailed 1960 Census occupation, industry, and class of worker categories (Duncan, 1961). Thus, our estimates of the quality of occupation reports do not pertain to descriptions of occupations per se, but to a particular transformation of detailed job descriptions into a status metric (Featherman and Hauser, 1973). Educational attainment is coded in exact years of schooling completed, and parental income is coded as the logarithm of price adjusted dollars.[2] The measure of weeks worked is computed from seven category midpoints; exact weeks worked, available for the ISR subsample, correlates .986 with this measure. Earned income in 1972 is computed as the natural logarithm of the sum of wage and salary, self-employed farm, and self-employed nonfarm income. Experience is computed as the number of years since the year the sample person started the first full-time civilian job he held after completing schooling.[3] The quadratic experience variable is computed as (experience - 20)^2/10. Working full-time and labor union membership are coded as dummy variables.

SPECIFICATION OF AN EARNINGS FUNCTION

We specify the following earnings function among true measures for nonblack males who report at least $1000 in 1973 earnings in the CPS interview:

$$LNEARN = \alpha + \beta_1 EX + \beta_2 FO + \beta_3 EX2 + \beta_4 FE + \beta_5 PI + \beta_6 ED$$

$$+ \beta_7 01 + \beta_8 OC + \beta_9 WKS + \beta_{10} FT + \beta_{11} UN + u, \qquad [1]$$

where the disturbance has the usual classical properties. We restrict the sample to those reporting at least $1000 in earnings for two reasons. First, men below that cut-off usually have marginal labor-force attachments and are likely to be subject to qualitatively different determinants of earnings. Second, reports of yearly earnings less than $1000 appear to be subject to disproportionately large errors of measurement (documentation available from authors on request).

The semilogarithmic form is specified for both substantive and methodological reasons. Human-capital theory suggests that the increase in earnings capacity due to a year of schooling is proportional to the earnings forgone during the year, and consequently the log of earnings capacity will be approximately a linear function of schooling (Mincer, 1974; Blinder, 1976). It is also reasonable to suppose that there is a constant proportionate return in earnings to a unit increase in the resources provided by social origins, rather than a constant dollar return.

Methodologically, using the logarithm of earnings allows for a more reasonable measurement model of response errors in reports of earnings, and it minimizes the effects of outliers which are often attributable to coding, keypunch, and transcription errors. One would expect the amount of error variation in earnings reports of those who earn, say, $35,000 to $40,000 to be considerably larger than the error variation in the reports of those who earn, say, $10,000 to $15,000. An additive measurement equation in the logarithm of earnings allows for this kind of heteroscedasticity in response errors (since it implies that error variation is a constant *proportion* of earnings), while an equation in dollar earnings requires that error variation be constant across levels of earnings. (Heteroscedasticity in conditional earnings distributions suggests a similar justification for using the logarithm of earnings in the structural equation.)

The effect of outliers on the correlation between two measures of dollar earnings can be quite dramatic. Our data suggest that a substantial proportion of the cases with reports of very large earnings involve coding or keypunch errors. Among the ISR subsample, 10 (of more than 800) respondents reported $40,000 or more in earnings in either the CPS interview or the ISR reinterview. In three of those ten cases, the interview and reinterview reports differ by more than $30,000 (the cross-tabulation is available from the authors on request). When these cases are included, the correlation between two reports of dollar earnings is .765, while the correlation between the reports of logarithmic earnings is .930. When the cases with at least $40,000 earnings are excluded, the correlation for dollar income is .976, for logarithmic income, .970. Clearly, the logarithmic measure is much less sensitive to the presence of the outliers. To further minimize their affects, we assign a value of $50,000 to all reports greater than that amount (yielding a correlation of .875 between two reports of dollar income, .940 between reports of logarithmic income).

The structural coefficients of the earnings function in equation 1 represent the net or direct effects of each of the determinants of earnings. However, we are also interested in the total and indirect effects of the determinants, especially of education and social origins. Consequently, we shall present estimates of reduced and semi-reduced forms as well as estimates of the structural form of equation 1. In doing so, we are assuming implicitly equation 1 to be imbedded in a larger block-recursive model with the following causal ordering:

$$
\begin{array}{l}
\text{EX} \\
\text{EX2} \qquad\qquad\qquad\qquad\quad \text{WKS} \\
\quad\Rightarrow \text{ED} \Rightarrow \text{01} \Rightarrow \text{OC} \Rightarrow \text{FT} \Rightarrow \text{LNEARN} \\
\text{FO} \qquad\qquad\qquad\qquad\quad\ \text{UN} \\
\text{FE} \\
\text{PI}
\end{array}
$$

The experience variables are considered exogenous because they represent cohort differences (year of entry to first job cohorts, rather than birth cohorts) as well as labor market experience per se.[4]

Our strategy is to specify and estimate a measurement model for the ISR and OCGR subsamples, and then to apply those estimates to the full CPS-OCGQ sample. In this way, we estimate substantive parameters in the full sample which have been corrected for response error. It is instructive to compare the corrected estimates with naive estimates for the full sample, i.e., estimates assuming perfect measurement. The models estimated in this paper apply to nonblack males in the experienced civilian labor force of March 1973 who reported at least $1000 in 1972 earned income in the March 1973 Current Population Survey. There are 24,352 nonblack males in the full CPS-OCGQ sample, 823 in the ISR subsample, and 556 in the OCGR subsample.

SPECIFICATION OF A MEASUREMENT MODEL

Our measurement model is presented in the path diagram of Figure 1. It shows the most general (least restricted) structure of response errors that we have estimated in the two subsamples. Ultimately, we eliminated all but two of the correlations among reporting errors. The variables enclosed in boxes (FO, FE, PI, O1, OC, WKS, LNEARN, EX, EX2, FT, UN) are unobserved true scores;[5] the last four are assumed to be measured without error.[6] The term x_{ij} refers to the measure of the ith variable obtained on the jth occasion, and e_{ij} is the error component of x_{ij}.

In algebraic form, the measurement model is:

$$x_{13} = \lambda_{13}FO + e_{13} \quad [2]$$
$$x_{14} = \lambda_{14}FT + e_{14} \quad [3]$$
$$x_{23} = \lambda_{23}FE + e_{23} \quad [4]$$
$$x_{24} = \lambda_{24}FE + e_{24} \quad [5]$$
$$x_{33} = \lambda_{33}PI + e_{33} \quad [6]$$
$$x_{34} = \lambda_{34}PI + e_{34} \quad [7]$$
$$x_{41} = \lambda_{41}ED + e_{41} \quad [8]$$
$$x_{43} = \lambda_{43}ED + e_{43} \quad [9]$$
$$x_{44} = \lambda_{44}ED + e_{44} \quad [10]$$
$$x_{53} = \lambda_{53}O1 + e_{53} \quad [11]$$
$$x_{54} = \lambda_{54}O1 + e_{54} \quad [12]$$
$$x_{61} = \lambda_{61}OC + e_{61} \quad [13]$$
$$x_{64} = \lambda_{64}OC + e_{64} \quad [14]$$
$$x_{71} = \lambda_{71}WKS + e_{71} \quad [15]$$
$$x_{72} = \lambda_{72}WKS + e_{72} \quad [16]$$
$$x_{81} = \lambda_{81}LNEARN + e_{81} \quad [17]$$
$$x_{82} = \lambda_{82}LNEARN + e_{82} \quad [18]$$

plus four identities: $x_{93} = EX$, $x_{10,3} = EX2$, $x_{11,1} = FT$, and $x_{12,3} = UN$.

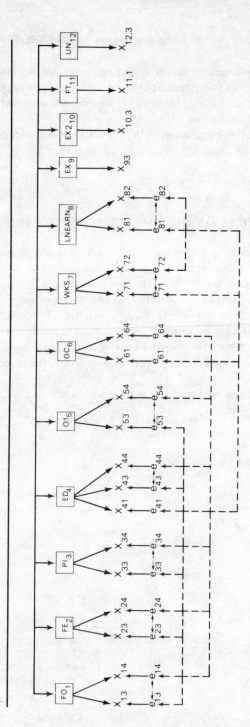

Note: Variables are defined in Table 1.

Figure 1: Measurement Model for Variables in an Earnings Function for Nonblack Males

To complete the model, the pattern of covariation among response errors must be specified. When multiple responses are obtained from the same individuals, three types of covariation among response errors appear particularly plausible. First, response errors in the report of a variable may covary with the respondent's true score on that variable. For example, individuals of high status may tend to understate their status while those of low status overstate their status. The implication for the measurement structure would be a nonunit slope of the population regression relating the observed measure, x_{ij}, to its corresponding true score, T_{ij}, while maintaining the lack of correlation between the true score and e_{ij}. A second source of covariation in response error would be a tendency for respondents to overstate the consistency between different variables ascertained on a single occasion. This "within-occasion between-variable correlated error" is represented in Figure 1 by the dotted lines showing correlations among the e_{i1}, for i=4, 6, 7, 8 (response errors of reports obtained from the March CPS household interview), among the e_{i2}, for i = 7, 8(response errors of reports obtained from the Spring ISR reinterview), among the e_{i3}, i = 1, 2, 3, 4, 5, (response errors of reports obtained from the Fall OCG questionnaire), and among the e_{i4}, for i = 1,2,3,4,5,6 (response errors of reports obtained from the Fall OCG remeasurement interview). A third source of correlated response error would be contamination of the respondent's report of a given variable by his recollection of his earlier report of that variable. It seems plausible that recall contamination might occur between CPS and ISR responses obtained about a week apart and between OCGQ and OCGR responses obtained about three weeks apart. The former within-variable between-occasion correlated error is represented in Figure 1 by correlations among pairs of response errors e_{i1} and e_{i2}, for i = 7,8, and the latter by correlations between e_{i3} and e_{i4}, for i = 1, . . . , 5. Note, however, that we assumed that recall contamination does not occur between the respective spring (CPS, ISR) and fall (OCGQ, OCGR) reports, obtained more than five months apart and often from different persons.

We establish a metric for the true scores by fixing $\lambda_{13}=\lambda_{23}=\lambda_{33}=\lambda_{41}=\lambda_{53}=\lambda_{61}=\lambda_{71}=\lambda_{81}=1.0$. That is, we fix the metric of the true scores to be the same as that of the observed reports which are used in models for the full CPS-OCGQ sample; the metrics of FO, FE, PI, and OI are identical to those of the corresponding OCGQ reports, and the CPS reports define the metrics for ED, OC, WKS, and LNEARN. Normalization of this kind is necessary because the metric of an unobserved variable is arbitrary, and consequently the slope coefficients with respect to indicators are identifiable only relative to each other. For example, given our normalization, a coefficient λ_{i2} greater (smaller) than unity indicates a slope of the ISR report on the corresponding true score which is steeper (flatter) than the slope of the CPS report on the true score. However, the absolute values of the two slopes are indeterminate. This normalization is imposed on all of our models. Another way of stating this normalization is that only the ratio of the slopes is identifiable. A more common normalization is to assume unit variances of true scores. However, this normalization does not allow the computation of metric coefficients relating unobservables. Error variances and reliabilities (squared true score-observed score correlations) are invariant with respect to normalization, although true-score variances (and structural coefficients) do depend on which λ_{ij} are fixed to unity.

Our measurement models are all based on equations 2 to 18. In order to estimate the parameters of all 17 measurement equations, we combine estimates of different subsets of equations from the ISR and OCGR subsamples. Within subsamples, we vary the specification of the covariances among the e_{ij} and the restrictions imposed on the λ_{ij}. We proceed by estimating and testing models in four stages, each involving a subsample and a subset of measurement equations. First, from the ISR subsample we estimate a three-variable, six-equation model for reports of education, weeks worked, and earnings. Second, we briefly discuss estimates for earners in the OCGR sample of the six-variable, thirteen-equation measurement model of social origins, education, and occupational attainments that has been examined in detail in our earlier research. In the third stage, we borrow the OCGR subsample estimates of measurement model parameters for equations 2, 4, 6, 11, and 13 (OCG reports of social origins and status of first job, and the CPS report of status of current job) so the measurement model in the ISR subsample can be extended to include social origins and occupational attainments. Similarly, in the fourth stage, we use the third-stage estimates of measurement model parameters for equations 15 (CPS report of weeks worked) and 17 (CPS report of earnings) to include weeks worked and earnings in a model for the OCGR subsample.

At each stage, we assess which correlations among reporting errors provide a significant improvement in fit over a model with random errors. We also look to see which λ_{ij} can be restricted to 1.0 without significantly altering the fit of the model. Our results from the four stages are then combined to provide point estimates of parameters in the full 17-equation measurement model. Finally, we use these estimates to correct the structural coefficients in equation 1 for measurement error in the full CPS-OCGQ sample.

ESTIMATION OF MEASUREMENT MODELS

Assuming the joint distribution of the reports of status variables is multivariate normal, we obtain maximum likelihood estimates of parameters of our measurement models using Jöreskog's (1970) general method for the analysis of covariance structures. The estimates have been computed from pairwise present correlations for nonblack males 20 to 65 years old in the experienced civilian labor force in March 1973 who reported at least $1000 in 1973 earned income in the CPS interview.[7] Correlations among the 11 measures to be used in estimating models from the ISR subsample appear in Table 2, and correlations among the 15 measures to be used in estimating models from the OCGR subsample appear in Table 3. Correlations for measures available in the full CPS-OCGQ sample appear in Table 4. Corresponding means and standard deviations appear in the first two columns of the top panel of Table 6, the bottom panel of Table 6, and Table 7, respectively. There are only a few notable differences in moments between the full sample and the two subsamples. The OCGR subsample is somewhat restricted in variation on weeks worked, earnings, and education (as reported in the CPS interview). It seems likely that the OCGR subsample disproportionately includes those with accurate earnings responses, since correlations between earnings and some other variables (particularly social origins and education) are notably higher in the OCGR subsample. The correlation between CPS and OCGQ reports of education is lowest in the OCGR subsample, and examination of cross-tabulations revealed that it is due to just a few outliers that happened to be selected into the OCGR subsample. The ISR subsample is somewhat restricted in variation on OCGQ reports of father's and respondent's education and exhibits slightly more variation in weeks worked than does the full CPS-OCGR sample. Correlations between the OCGQ education report and other variables are generally higher in the ISR subsample, suggesting that those giving more accurate OCGQ education reports were disproportionately included in the ISR subsample. (The error variation in the OCGQ report estimated from the ISR subsample is substantially lower than that estimated from the OCGQ subsample.) Curiously, the correlations between earnings and weeks worked are unusually high in the ISR subsample (about .54) and low in the OCGR subsample (.37). It should be stressed, however, that we have focused on the largest discrepancies, and subsample moments are subject to considerably more sampling variability than are the full sample moments.

Goodness-of-fit tests for our various measurement models appear in Table 5. The likelihood-ratio test statistic contrasts the null hypothesis that constraints on the observed variance-covariance matrix are satisfied in the population with the alternative that the variance-covariance matrix is unrestricted. In large samples, this statistic has a chi-square distribution with degrees of freedom equal to the difference between the number of variances and covariances and the number of independent parameters estimated under the hypothesized model. Moreover, when two measurement models are nested, that is, when one model can be obtained by constraining the parameters of a more general model, the difference in chi-square values provides a likelihood-ratio test of the constraints on the parameters.

Goodness-of-fit tests for six-equation, three-variable models of education, weeks worked, and earnings—estimated from the ISR subsample—are presented in the top panel of Table 5. Each model is based on equations 8, 9, 15, 16, 17, and 18. Our simplest model assumes mutually uncorrelated errors and no restrictions (other than the normalizations) on the λ_{ij}. This model corresponds to the random-measurement error models of Siegel and Hodge (1968: 51-52), Jencks et al. (1972: 330-336), Treiman and Hauser (1977), and the one implicitly used by other researchers applying "corrections for attenuation" (see Bohrnstedt, 1970). The 21 observable variances and covariances among the 6 measures provide more than enough information to identify the 15 unknown model parameters: 3 true score variances, 3 true score covariances, 6 error variances, and 3 slope coefficients (λ_{ij}). The χ^2 value of 28.02 with 6 degrees of freedom (p = .000) on line 1A suggests that the restrictions on observable moments implied by the random-error model probably do not hold in the population. Model 1B introduces the three within-occasion correlations among response errors in CPS reports of education, weeks worked, and earnings, and the single correlation between response errors in ISR reports of weeks worked and earnings. Contrasting line 1B with line 1A, it is clear that adding the

TABLE 2

Observed Correlations among Variables Measured in CPS Interview, Income Supplement Reinterview, and OCG Questionnaire: ISR Subsample of Nonblack Males in the March 1973 Experienced Civilian Labor Force Reporting Earnings of at least $1000 in the CPS (N=823)

Variable	Measure	(1) x_{13}	(2) x_{23}	(3) x_{33}	(4) x_{41}	x_{43}	(5) x_{53}	(6) x_{61}	(7) x_{71}	x_{72}	(8) x_{81}	x_{82}
1. FO	x_{13}	--										
2. FE	x_{23}	.547	--									
3. PI	x_{33}	.408	.405	--								
4. ED	x_{41}	.406	.438	.438	--							
	x_{43}	.389	.429	.460	.884	--						
5. OI	x_{53}	.420	.330	.332	.673	.682	--					
6. OC	x_{61}	.331	.283	.293	.584	.585	.634	--				
7. WKS	x_{71}	-.096	-.055	-.036	.037	.053	.055	.151	--			
	x_{72}	-.101	-.044	-.032	.061	.073	.054	.146	.940	--		
8. LNEARN	x_{81}	.080	.055	.127	.276	.301	.339	.429	.540	.544	--	
	x_{82}	.172	.077	.139	.293	.299	.345	.441	.550	.571	.940	--

NOTE: See Table 1 for definition of variables.

TABLE 3

Observed Correlates among Variables Measured in CPS Interview, OCG Questionnaire, and OCG Remeasurement Interview: OCGR Subsample of Nonblack Males in the March 1973 Experienced Civilian Labor Force Reporting Earnings of at least $1000 in the CPS (N=556)

Variable	Measure	(1)		(2)		(3)		(4)			(5)		(6)		(7)	(8)
		x_{13}	x_{14}	x_{23}	x_{24}	x_{33}	x_{34}	x_{41}	x_{42}	x_{43}	x_{53}	x_{54}	x_{61}	x_{64}	x_{71}	x_{81}
1. FO	x_{13}	--														
	x_{14}	.872	--													
2. FE	x_{23}	.579	.573	--												
	x_{24}	.591	.586	.937	--											
3. PI	x_{33}	.410	.415	.459	.453	--										
	x_{34}	.414	.428	.467	.463	.909	--									
4. ED	x_{41}	.408	.406	.458	.460	.467	.483	--								
	x_{42}	.424	.424	.449	.447	.412	.426	.795	--							
	x_{43}	.437	.436	.482	.492	.474	.492	.919	.835	--						
5. OI	x_{53}	.392	.411	.292	.301	.362	.351	.635	.578	.642	--					
	x_{54}	.401	.410	.324	.321	.360	.345	.636	.580	.644	.847	--				
6. OC	x_{61}	.370	.404	.309	.326	.315	.311	.577	.521	.602	.614	.617	--			
	x_{64}	.345	.382	.298	.302	.288	.296	.540	.500	.560	.578	.595	.801	--		
7. WKS	x_{71}	-.065	-.043	-.061	-.035	-.039	-.018	.071	.017	.068	.002	.031	.148	.133	--	
8. LNEARN	x_{81}	.184	.183	.132	.118	.168	.176	.363	.319	.368	.321	.346	.450	.398	.373	--

NOTE: See Table 1 for definition of variables.

TABLE 4

Observed Correlations among Variables Measured in CPS Interview and OCG Questionnaire: Full CPS-OCGQ Sample of Nonblack Males in the March 1973 Experienced Civilian Labor Force Reporting Earnings of at Least $1000 in the CPS (N=24,352)

Variable	Measure	(1) x_{13}	(2) x_{23}	(3) x_{33}	(4) x_{41}	x_{43}	(5) x_{53}	(6) x_{61}	(7) x_{71}	(8) x_{81}	(9) x_{93}	(10) $x_{10,3}$	(11) $x_{11,1}$	(12) $x_{12,3}$
1. FO	x_{13}	--												
2. FE	x_{23}	.531	--											
3. PI	x_{33}	.423	.434	--										
4. ED	x_{41}	.408	.468	.431	--									
	x_{43}	.388	.461	.420	.853	--								
5. O1	x_{53}	.395	.331	.309	.636	.621	--							
6. OC	x_{61}	.334	.277	.285	.572	.542	.621	--						
7. WKS	x_{71}	-.027	-.037	.005	.034	.043	.066	.140	--					
8. LNEARN	x_{81}	.107	.060	.145	.264	.271	.310	.411	.437	--				
9. EX	x_{93}	-.224	-.349	-.273	-.382	-.370	-.237	-.100	.138	.149	--			
10. EX2	$x_{10,3}$	-.014	-.028	-.087	-.148	-.150	-.102	-.105	-.114	-.240	.304	--		
11. FT	$x_{11,1}$	-.071	-.076	-.037	-.046	-.007	.023	.045	.182	.331	.110	-.142	--	
12. UN1OW	$x_{12,3}$	-.134	-.113	-.096	-.197	-.197	-.242	-.287	-.013	.042	.077	-.015	.053	--

NOTE: See Table 1 for definition of variables.

TABLE 5
Chi-square Goodness-of-fit Tests for Measurement Models: Nonblack Males in the Experienced Civilian Labor Force, March 1973, Who Reported at Least $1000 in Earnings in the Current Population Survey

Model	χ^2	df	p
1. Three-variable ISR model (N=823)			
A. Random measurement error--no slope restrictions	28.02	6	.000
B. Within-occasion correlated errors $\rho_{e_{41},e_{71}}$, $\rho_{e_{41},e_{81}}$, $\rho_{e_{71},e_{81}}$, $\rho_{e_{72},e_{82}}$	3.62	2	.163
C. Within-occasion correlated errors $\rho_{e_{41},e_{81}}$ and $\rho_{e_{72},e_{82}}$	5.44	4	.246
D. Within-occasion correlated error $\rho_{e_{72},e_{82}}$	14.29	5	.014
E. Within-occasion correlated errors $\rho_{e_{41},e_{81}}$ and $\rho_{e_{72},e_{82}}$ and 12 slope restrictions	5.88	6	.437
2. Six-variable OCGR model (N=556)			
Random measurement error and 5 slope restrictions	40.78	55	.923
3. Eight-variable ISR model (N=823)			
A. Random measurement error and 2 slope restrictions	48.69	23	.001
B. Within-occasion correlated errors $\rho_{e_{41},e_{81}}$ and $\rho_{e_{72},e_{82}}$ and 2 slope restrictions	23.91	21	.297
C. Within-occasion correlated error $\rho_{e_{72},e_{82}}$ and 2 slope restrictions	30.61	22	.104
4. Eight-variable OCGR model (N=556)			
A. Random measurement error and 5 slope restrictions	58.14	69	.821
B. Within-occasion correlated errors $\rho_{e_{41},e_{71}}$; $\rho_{e_{41},e_{81}}$; $\rho_{e_{61},e_{71}}$; and $\rho_{e_{61},e_{81}}$; and 5 slope restrictions	56.34	65	.769
C. Random measurement error except $\rho_{e_{41},e_{81}}$ fixed at -.14 and 5 slope restrictions	60.12	69	.768

a. Maximum likelihood estimates were computed with the ACOVSF program described in Joreskog, Gruvaeus and van Thillo (1970).

four within-occasion error correlations significantly improves the fit of the measurement model. We reduce χ^2 by more than 24 points while using only 4 more degrees of freedom. Furthermore, two of the four error correlations are not significantly larger than their standard errors. Model 1C introduces only the two larger error correlations, $\rho_{e_{41}, e_{81}}$ and $\rho_{e_{72}, e_{82}}$. Contrasting line 1C with line 1B, we see that nearly all of the improvement in fit can be attributed to these two error correlations: a negative correlation of -.17 between response errors in CPS reports in education and earnings, and a positive correlation of .33 between errors in ISR reports of weeks worked and earnings (their respective standard errors are .07 and .08). Since a tendency for respondents to understate the consistency between their education and earnings in the CPS can have a substantial effect on estimated returns to schooling, we want to be relatively certian that the correlation $\rho_{e_{41}, e_{81}}$ does indeed contribute to the fit of the model. Consequently, we estimate a model where $\rho_{e_{41}, e_{81}}$ is constrained to equal zero while $\rho_{e_{72}, e_{82}}$ remains in the model. Contrasting lines 1D and 1C, it is clear that $\rho_{e_{41}, e_{81}}$ makes a statistically significant contribution to the fit (eliminating $\rho_{e_{41}, e_{81}}$ increases χ^2 by 8.85 and adds 1 degree of freedom, $p > .005$). Finally, two of the three free λ_{ij} were estimated to be nearly 1.0. However λ_{43} was estimated to be 1.08 (with a standard error of .02). Thus, as our earlier research based on the OCGR subsample has shown, the slope of the OCGQ report of education on the true score appears significantly steeper than the slope for the CPS report. Model 1E, imposing $\lambda_{72} = \lambda_{82} = 1.0$, increases the χ^2 value marginally over that of 1C, while adding two degrees of freedom. Thus, in the third stage, we combine the specification of model 1E with selected parameters estimated within the OCGR subsample.

While we have been able to test for the presence of some types of correlated error in the ISR subsample, we have not been able to test for the presence of the plausible within-variable error correlations involving weeks worked and income ($\rho_{e_{71}, e_{72}}, \rho_{e_{81}, e_{82}}$). These are not identified in any of the ISR subsample models examined here. Therefore, neither can any such correlations be detected, nor could they affect the fit of the measurement model. However, within-variable error correlations may affect estimated structural relations among true variables, and we shall consider this possibility below.

Next, we briefly discuss the six-variable, thirteen-equation measurement model for social origins, education, and occupational attainments. The specification of Model 2 is identical to that of the final measurement model for nonblack males developed in our earlier research

(Bielby et al., 1977a): mutually uncorrelated response errors and two free slope parameters, $\lambda_{43} = \lambda_{44}$ and λ_{64}. The present estimates for Model 2 differ from those reported elsewhere because males reporting less than $1000 in earnings in the CPS (22 cases) have been excluded from the subsample. The 36 parameters of Model 2 do remarkably well in representing the 91 variances and covariances among the reports (χ^2 = 40.78 with 55 degrees of freedom, p = .923). Direct tests and indirect evidence of the extent of within-occasion and within-variable correlations among reporting errors are presented in our earlier paper. We found virtually no evidence of any error correlations. Point estimates of measurement parameters based on the 556 OCGR earners are nearly identical to those estimated previously from the 578 OCGR males in the experienced civilian labor force. Thus, in the fourth stage, we combine the specification of Model 2 with selected parameters estimated in the third stage.

In the third stage of estimation and specification, we add equations 2, 4, 6, 11, and 13 for OCGQ reports of education and first job status, and the CPS report of current job status to the specification of Model 1E in order to obtain an eight-variable, eleven-equation model which can be estimated in the ISR subsample. Error variances of e_{13}, e_{23}, e_{33}, e_{53}, and e_{61} are borrowed from the second stage results (Model 2), and appear in column 3 of the top panel of Table 6. Relying on Model 2, we assume mutually uncorrelated response errors among reports of social origins, schooling, and occupational achievements. Model 3A assumes all errors to be mutually uncorrelated, constrains λ_{72} and λ_{82} to equal 1.0, but leaves λ_{43} unconstrained. The 11 reports provide 66 observed moments from which to solve for 43 parameters: 8 true score variances, 28 true score covariances, 6 error variances (two others are known), and one slope coefficient. The χ^2 value of 48.69 with 23 degrees of freedom (p = .001) indicates that, as expected (given the results of Model 1A), the restrictions on observable moments implied by Model 3A probably do not hold in the population. (The degrees of freedom are not strictly correct, since the five borrowed error variances are sample estimates, not known population parameters. Nevertheless, differences in degrees of freedom for nested models are correct.) Model 3B introduces the two error correlations, $\rho_{e_{41},e_{81}}$ and $\rho_{e_{72},e_{82}}$, detected in Model 1C. Contrasting line 3B with line 3A, we again see a significant improvement to fit due to the two within-occasion error correlations; χ^2 drops by nearly 25 points, using only 2 degrees of freedom, (p < .001). Point estimates of the error correlations are -.14 and .37 (their respective standard errors are .05 and .09). To further examine the degree to which $\rho_{e_{41},e_{81}}$ contributes to the fit of the model, we estimate Model 3C where it is constrained to equal zero while $\rho_{e_{72},e_{82}}$ remains in the model. Contrasting lines 3C with 3B, we again find that $\rho_{e_{41}, e_{81}}$ makes a statistically significant contribution to the fit; eliminating $\rho_{e_{41}, e_{81}}$ increases χ^2 by 6.70 and adds one degree of freedom ($p < .01$). Thus, we accept Model 3B as the final measurement model estimated from the ISR subsample. Parameter estimates for Model 3B appear in the top panel of Table 6. They are discussed in detail below.

In the fourth stage, we add equations 15 and 17 for CPS reports of weeks worked and earnings to the specification of Model 2 in order to obtain an eight-variable, fifteen-equation model to be estimated in the OCGR subsample. Error variances of e_{71} and e_{81} are borrowed from the third-stage results (Model 3B) and appear in column 3 of the bottom panel of Table 6. Relying on the results reported above, we allow just two free slope parameters, λ_{64} and $\lambda_{42} = \lambda_{43}$. In Model 4A, we specify all fifteen response error terms to be mutually uncorrelated. In that model, the 15 reports provide 120 observed moments from which to solve for 51 model parameters: 8 true score variances, 28 true score covariances, 13 error variances (two others are known), and two slope coefficients. The χ^2 value of 58.14 with 69 degrees of freedom ($p = .821$) indicates that the restrictions implied by Model 4A provide a reasonable fit to the observable moments. (As in the third-stage models, the degrees of freedom are not strictly correct, since two of the "known" fixed parameters, $\sigma_{e_{71}}$ and $\sigma_{e_{81}}$, are actually estimates from the OCGR subsample). In model 4B, we add four within-occasion correlations among errors in CPS reports. Two of the four, $\rho_{e_{41},e_{71}}$ and $\rho_{e_{41},e_{81}}$, were identified and estimated in the ISR subsample, and we detected a statistically significant effect of the latter. The other two, $\rho_{e_{61},e_{71}}$ and $\rho_{e_{71},e_{81}}$, were not estimated in the ISR subsample. Contrasting lines 4B and 4A, it is clear that the four error correlations contribute virtually no improvement to the fit of the model, decreasing χ^2 by only 1.80 while using four degrees of freedom ($p > .75$). Indeed, if a decrease of that amount could be attributed to just one of the error correlations, it would not be statistically significant (i.e., $p > .10$ for $\chi^2 = 1.80$ with one degree of freedom). Thus, the fourth-stage OCGR models do not replicate the finding from the ISR subsample of a significant negative correlation among reporting errors in CPS reports of education and earnings. The point estimate of $\rho_{e_{41},e_{81}}$ in Model 4B is .085, compared to $\hat{\rho}_{e_{41},e_{81}} = -.14$ under Model 3B. Model 4C, which is identical to Model 4A except that

TABLE 6
Observed Moments and Measurement Model Parameter Estimates: Nonblack Males in the Experienced Civilian Labor Force, March 1973, Who Reported at Least $1000 in the Current Population Survey

Income Supplement Reinterview (N=813)

Variable	Measure	(1) Mean $\bar{\mu}_{ij}$	(2) Observed Std. Dev. σ_{ij}	(3) Std. Dev. of Error[a] $\sigma_{e_{ij}}$	(4) Relative Slope[a] λ_{ij}	(5) Reliability Coefficient $(\sigma^2_{T_i}/\sigma^2_{x_{ij}})\lambda^2_{ij}$	(6) Percent of Cases with Data Present
1. FO	x_{13}	32.74	23.78	9.26	1.00	.848	95
	x_{14}	--	--	--	--	--	--
2. FE	x_{23}	9.055	3.895	1.14	1.00	.914	94
	x_{24}	--	--	--	--	--	--
3. PI	x_{33}	8.750	.8637	0.32	1.00	.861	90
	x_{34}	--	--	--	--	--	--
4. ED	x_{41}	12.33	3.019	1.08 (.06)	1.00	.872	100[b]
	x_{43}	12.19	3.220	1.03 (.07)	1.08 (.02)	.897	94
	x_{44}	--	--	--	--	--	--
5. OI	x_{53}	35.51	25.12	9.93	1.00	.845	88
	x_{54}	--	--	--	--	--	--
6. OC	x_{61}	43.24	25.44	9.82	1.00	.850	100[b]
	x_{64}	--	--	--	--	--	--
7. WKS	x_{71}	47.89	8.898	2.38 (.17)	1.00	.927	100[b]
	x_{72}	47.87	8.784	1.93 (.20)	--	.953	97
8. LNEARN	x_{81}	9.130	.6389	0.178 (.011)	1.00	.922	100[b]
	x_{82}	9.136	.6266	0.128 (.014)	--	.958	93

OCG Remeasurement Subsample (N=556)

Variable	Measure	(1) Mean $\bar{\mu}_{ij}$	(2) Observed Std. Dev. σ_{ij}	(3) Std. Dev. of Error[a] $\sigma_{e_{ij}}$	(4) Relative Slope[a] λ_{ij}	(5) Reliability Coefficient $(\sigma^2_{T_i}/\sigma^2_{x_{ij}})\lambda^2_{ij}$	(6) Percent of Cases with Data Present
1. FO	x_{13}	32.73	24.21	9.22 (.55)	1.00	.854	96
	x_{14}	33.29	23.54	7.83 (.60)	1.00	.889	95
2. FE	x_{23}	8.930	4.139	1.14 (.09)	1.00	.923	95
	x_{24}	8.904	4.093	0.91 (.10)	1.00	.951	94
3. PI	x_{33}	8.710	.9323	0.32 (.021)	1.00	.876	89
	x_{34}	8.773	.8943	0.21 (.028)	1.00	.943	90
4. ED	x_{41}	12.18	2.821	0.97 (.04)	1.00	.884	100[b]
	x_{43}	12.01	3.407	1.78 (.06)	1.07 (.02)	.717	94
	x_{44}	12.16	2.903	0.60 (.06)	1.07 (.02)	.956	96
5. OI	x_{53}	34.86	24.77	9.89 (.54)	1.00	.839	90
	x_{54}	32.31	24.28	9.30 (.55)	1.00	.856	95
6. OC	x_{61}	41.69	25.26	9.52 (.81)	1.00	.837	100[b]
	x_{64}	39.91	24.87	12.44 (.62)	0.92 (.04)	.749	100[b]
7. WKS	x_{71}	48.58	7.165	2.38	1.00	.889	100[b]
	x_{72}	--	--	--	--	--	--
8. LNEARN	x_{81}	9.150	.5753	0.178	1.00	.904	100[b]
	x_{82}	--	--	--	--	--	--

a. Approximate standard errors of parameter estimates appear in parentheses.
b. Missing values have been allocated for NA cases.
c. In the ISR subsample, $\rho_{e41, e81} = -.14$, $\rho_{e72, e82} = .37$.
d. In the OCGR subsample, response errors were specified to be mutually uncorrelated.

$\rho_{e_{41},e_{81}}$ is fixed at $-.14$, provides a worse fit than Model 4A. However, the comparison of fourth stage OCGR models are not quite as conclusive as they may appear. The error correlations in question are affected by parameter estimates borrowed from the ISR subsample. Consequently, sampling error in the borrowed estimates and differential selection bias in the two subsamples may have reduced our ability to detect these particular within-variable error correlations.[8]

Model 4A is our final measurement model in the OCGR subsample, and Model 3B is our final measurement model in the ISR subsample. Together, they provide at least one point estimate of every parameter in the 17-equation measurement model (see Table 6), but they provide substantially different estimates for two of those parameters. One is the response error variation in the OCGQ report of educational attainment; $\sigma_{e_{43}}$ is estimated as 1.03 years from the ISR subsample and 1.78 years from the OCGR subsample. This difference is rather large relative to the respective standard errors of the variance components. As we noted above, the OCGR subsample contained a disproportionate number of cases with large discrepancies between CPS and OCGQ reports of educational attainment, while those with more accurate OCGQ responses seemed disproportionately represented in the ISR subsample. This appears to account for the different estimates. Furthermore, this discrepancy will not affect bias due to our assessment of response errors in the earnings function, for only the CPS report of education is used in estimating equation 1.

The discrepancy in estimates of $\rho_{e_{41},e_{81}}$ is more serious because it affects estimates of the returns to schooling. In our "listwise" estimates for the ISR subsample (excluding the 290 cases with any missing or allocated responses), we detected no such error correlation, suggesting that it might be an artifact of either the census allocation procedure or of the pairwise present computing scheme.[9] Nor was the error correlation detected in (pairwise) ISR-subsample estimates using dollar income rather than logarithmic income. Because of the ambiguous status of the negative correlation between errors in CPS reports of education and earnings, in assessing biases due to response errors, we will first assume that the error correlation is zero and then assess the effect of an error correlation of $-.14$.

Within-variable, between-occasion correlations among response errors, for example, contamination of a later report of a variable by recall of an earlier report, have not been discussed in detail. As noted above, our earlier research (Bielby et al., 1977a) has produced strong evidence that no such correlations exist among errors in reports of social origins, education, and occupational attainments. Given those results, there appears to be no prima facie reason why such correlations should be presumed to exist among reports of either weeks worked or earnings. Nevertheless, we assess below the effect on estimates of the earnings function of a within-variable correlation between errors in reports of earnings, $\rho_{e_{81},e_{82}}$, as high as 0.5. A value of $\rho_{e_{81},e_{82}}$ greater than zero would increase estimates of $\sigma_{e_{81}}$ and $\sigma_{e_{82}}$ (and therefore lower reliabilities of earnings below levels reported in Table 6). Since it would leave the covariance between e_{41} and e_{81} unchanged, it would decrease the estimate of $\rho_{e_{41},e_{81}}$. All other estimates would remain unchanged, as would the tests of models in Table 5.

Estimates in Table 6 of measurement model parameters involving social origins, education, and occupational achievements are nearly identical to those reported in our earlier research. OCGR remeasurement interview reports have uniformly lower error variances than corresponding OCGR questionnaire reports, and social origins appear to be measured no less accurately than socioeconomic achievements. Both ISR and OCGR subsample estimates show the regression of the CPS report of education on the true score to be flatter than the regression for the OCGQ report.[10] The CPS report of current occupational status has a steeper slope than does the fall remeasurement report.

The Income Supplement Reinterview, conducted by experienced census personnel, often in person, appears to be more accurate than the CPS interview. Error variation ($\hat{\sigma}_{e_{ii}}$) in the reinterview report of weeks worked is about 20% lower than that in the CPS report, and error variation in the reinterview report of earnings is nearly 30% lower than that in the CPS report. The standard deviation of errors in CPS reports of earnings is 17.8%; that is, the error variation is predicted to be $890 for true earnings of $5000, $1780 for true earnings of $10,000, and $4,450 for true earnings of $25,000. The standard deviation of errors in ISR reports of earnings is 12.8%, which implies error variations of $640, $1280, and $3200 at the respective true levels of earnings cited above. In contrast, a measurement model in dollar earnings yields estimates of $2450 and $2330 for error variation in CPS and ISR reports, respectively, regardless of the level of earnings; as noted earlier, the data are not consistent with the assumption of constant error variation in dollar earnings. Moreover, the estimates based on dollar earnings suggest there is more error in earnings near the middle of the earnings distribution ($9000 to $11,000) than do the estimates based on our semilogarithmic specification.

To summarize, response errors in reports of socioeconomic variables by nonblack males appear to be almost completely random. Respondents appear to overstate the consistency between earnings and weeks worked in the Income Supplement Reinterview, and less conclusive results suggest that they may understate the consistency between CPS reports of educational attainment and earnings. Overall, retrospective reports of social origins by nonblack males are about as accurate as reports of their own educational attainments and socioeconomic achievements. Estimates of a 17-equation measurement model obtained from the ISR and OCGR subsamples can now be applied to the full CPS-OCGQ sample in order to assess the biases in the coefficients of an earnings function that are attributable to response error.

ESTIMATION OF AN EARNINGS FUNCTION IN THE FULL CPS-OCGQ SAMPLE

Estimates from the two subsamples of parameters of measurement model equations 2, 4, 6, 8, 11, 13, 15, and 17 are used to obtain corrected full-sample moments among variables entering the earnings function (equation 1). By computing the earnings function from both corrected and uncorrected full-sample moments we can assess the extent to which response errors bias estimates of the coefficients of equation 1.[11]

Estimates of measurement model parameters for social origins (equations 2, 4, and 6), and occupational attainments (equations 11 and 13) are taken from OCGR subsample Model 4A; that is, they are selected from the bottom panel of Table 6. Estimates of measurement model parameters for weeks worked and earnings (equations 15 and 17) are taken from ISR subsample Model 3B; that is they are selected from the top panel of Table 6. Estimates of measurement model parameters for educational attainment (equation 8) are pooled from both subsamples. Since the λ_{ij} are normalized to 1.0 for all reports used to estimate the earnings function in the full sample, only estimates of the error variation (σe_{ij}) and ρe_{41}, e_{81} need be taken from Table 6. The estimates of error variation appear in column 3 of Table 7; $\hat{\sigma} e_{41}$ is the average of the OCGR and ISR estimates weighted by the inverse of their respective standard errors. Under the specification of the measurement model, the true score variances are computed as the observed variances in the full sample less the corresponding response error variances from the subsamples (column 4 of Table 7). Except for the covariance of educational attainment and earnings, the true score covariances are set equal to the

TABLE 7

Full CPS—OCGQ Sample Observed Moments (N=24,352), Subsample Estimates of Standard Deviations of Errors, and Combined Estimates of True Standard Deviations: Nonblack Males in the Experienced Civilian Labor Force, March 1973, Who Reported Earnings of at Least $1000 in the Current Population Survey (N=24,352)

		(1) Mean $\hat{\mu}_{ij}$	(2) Observed Std. Dev. $\hat{\sigma}_{x_{ij}}$	(3) Std. Dev. of Error $\hat{\sigma}_{e_{ij}}$	(4) Std. Dev. of True Score $\hat{\sigma}_{T_{ij}}$	(5) Percent of Cases with Data Present
Variable	Measure					
1. FO	x_{13}	31.02	22.90	9.22	20.96	94
2. FE	x_{23}	8.775	4.020	1.14	3.855	94
3. PI	x_{33}	8.683	.9210	0.32	.8636	90
4. ED	x_{41}	12.10	3.050	1.01	2.878	100[a]
	x_{43}	11.96	3.402	--	--	94
5. OI	x_{53}	34.00	24.68	9.89	22.61	88
6. OC	x_{61}	41.53	25.02	9.52	23.14	100[a]
7. WKS	x_{71}	47.93	8.416	2.38	8.072	100[a]
8. LNEARN	x_{81}	9.093	.6534	0.178	.6287	100[a]
9. EX	$x_{9,3}$	19.65	13.44	--	--	99
10. EX2	$x_{10,3}$	18.07	17.81	--	--	99
11. FT	$x_{11,1}$	0.964	0.186	--	--	100
12. UN	$x_{12,3}$	0.305	0.460	--	--	99

a. Missing values have been allocated for NA cases.

observed full-sample covariance. Under the specification $\rho_{e_{41},e_{81}} = 0$, the true score covariance of education and earnings is also equal to the observed full-sample covariance. Under the specification $\rho_{e_{41},e_{81}} = -.14$ the true score covariance is equal to the observed full-sample covariance less the estimated covariance of the errors (where the latter is $\rho_{e_{41},e_{81}} \sigma_{e_{41}} \sigma_{e_{81}}$). The corrected correlations obtained from the true score variances and covariances are given in Table 8.

Table 9 presents corrected estimates of structural- and reduced-form parameters of the earnings function under the assumption that response

TABLE 8
Corrected Correlations: Full CPS-OCGQ Sample of Nonblack Males in the March 1973 Experienced Civilian Labor Force Reporting Earnings of at Least $1000 in the CPS (N=24,352)

Variable	(1)	(2)	(3)	(4)	(5)	(6)	(7)	(8)	(9)	(10)	(11)	(12)
1. FO	--											
2. FE	.605	--										
3. PI	.493	.483	--									
4. ED	.472	.517	.488	--								
5. O1	.471	.377	.360	.736	--							
6. OC	.395	.312	.329	.656	.733	--						
7. WKS	-.031	-.040	-.006	.038	.075	.158	--					
8. LNEARN	.121	.065	.161	***b,c	.352	.462	.474	--				
9. EX	-.245	-.364	-.291	-.405	-.259	-.108	.144	.155	--			
10. EX2	-.015	-.029	-.093	-.157	-.111	-.114	-.119	-.249	.304	--		
11. FT	-.078	-.079	-.039	-.049	.025	.049	.190	.344	.110	-.142	--	
12. UN	-.146	-.118	-.101	-.209	-.264	-.310	-.014	.044	.077	-.015	.053	--

a. Correlations have been corrected with measurement model parameters estimated from subsamples of 823 (ISR) and 556 (COGR) observations.

b. $\rho_{ed1, e81} = .291$ when $\rho_{ed1, e81} = 0.00$

c. $\rho_{ed1, e81} = .305$ when $\rho_{ed1, e81} = -.14.$

errors are random. Metric and standardized coefficients are presented for the structural form (line 6), and reduced forms of the earnings function (lines 1 through 5). In addition, a simple schooling and experience function is estimated (line 7), and the bivariate schooling regression is presented (line 8).

The first reduced-form equation in Table 9 reveals that while each of the three social origin variables has an independent effect on earnings, parental income (PI) has by far the largest effect with an elasticity of nearly .12. The total effect of father's occupational status (FO) is about 2% for 10 SEI points, and the effect of a year of father's education (FE) is 0.76%. The experience variables (EX, EX2) have the largest relative impact on earnings, and the earnings-experience profile, net of social origins, peaks at about 27 years of experience.[12]

Education (ED) mediates virtually all of the effects of FO and FE (cf. lines 2 and 1), but nearly half of the effect of parental income is not mediated by schooling. That is, father's occupational status and father's educational attainment affect earnings by increasing or decreasing the length of schooling, but the financial status of the family of origin affects earnings both through schooling and in other ways. The total return to a year of schooling, net of experience, and social origins is more than 8%. Overall, schooling, experience, and social origins account for over one-fourth of the variance in earnings.

In line 3, we find that there is almost an 8% return to 10 SEI points of first job status (01), net of education, experience, and social origins, with 01 mediating about one-half the return to schooling, but none of the effect of parental income. There is a 9% return to 10 SEI points of current job status (line 4), with OC mediating more than half the return to first job status. The return to schooling net of both occupational statuses is less than 2%, but the elasticity of parental income remains almost .06. Schooling, experience, social origins, and occupational achievements account for over one-third of the variance in earnings.

On line 5, we find a 2.74 return to each additional week worked (WKS), the largest effect relative to those of the other variables in the earnings equation (cf. standardized coefficients). Labor supply, as indicated by WKS, mediates about 20% of the effect of experience, probably through the decreased labor supply of older workers. WKS mediates a little less than 20% of the effect of current occupation.

The full equation (line 7) accounts for over half the variance in the log of earnings. Net of all other variables in the model, union members

TABLE 9

Corrected Estimates of an Earnings Function for 1972 Earned Income (LINEARN), Assuming Random Errors: Nonblack Males in the Experienced Civilian Labor Force, March 1973, Who Reported at Least $1000 in the Current Population Survey (N=24,352).

Equation	EX	EX2	FO[b]	FE	PI	ED	O1[b]	OC[b]	WKS	FT	UN	R^2	Residual σ_u	Explained σ_t	Total σ_t
						Predetermined Variables								Components of Variation[a]	
1.	.0161 (.344)	-.0118 (-.336)	.0277 (.092)	.0076 (.046)	.118 (.162)	--	--	--	--	--	--	.177	.570	.264	.6285
2.	.0195 (.417)	-.0109 (-.309)	.0079 (.026)	-.0069 (-.043)	.053 (.076)	.0841 (.385)	--	--	--	--	--	.266	.538	.324	
3.	.0189 (.405)	-.0108 (-.305)	-.0103 (-.034)	-.0029 (-.018)	.062 (.085)	.0407 (.186)	.0773 (.278)	--	--	--	--	.299	.526	.344	
4.	.0161 (.344)	-.0101 (-.285)	-.0151 (-.050)	-.0017 (-.010)	.056 (.077)	.0175 (.080)	.0291 (.105)	.0910 (.335)	--	--	--	.345	.509	.369	
5.	.0128 (.273)	-.0081 (-.229)	-.0078 (-.026)	-.0020 (-.012)	.050 (.069)	.0184 (.084)	.0285 (.103)	.0736 (.271)	.0274 (.352)	--	--	.459	.462	.426	
6.	.0112 (.239)	-.0065 (-.185)	-.0030 (-.010)	-.0020 (-.012)	.046 (.063)	.0216 (.099)	.0261 (.094)	.0840 (.309)	.0248 (.319)	.707 (.210)	.220 (.161)	.527	.432	.456	
7.	.0194 (.416)	-.0110 (-.311)	--	--	--	.0897 (.411)	--	--	--	--	--			.321	
8.	--	--	--	--	--	.0635 (.291)	--	--	--	--	--			.183	

NOTE: Standardized coefficients appear in parentheses. Estimates of error variances are based on subsamples of 823 (ISR) and 556 (OCGR) observations.

a. Components are expressed as standard deviations. The additive decomposition was $\sigma_t^2 = \sigma_t^2 + \sigma_u^2$.

b. Variables expressed in the metric of Duncan SEI scores have been divided by 10 and corresponding coefficients multiplied by 10.

(UN) earn about 25% more than nonmembers ($e^{.22}=1.25$), and those employed full-time (FT) earn about twice as much as those working part-time ($e^{.707}=2.03$). The net return to an additional week worked is 2.5% in the full equation, and the return to 10 SEI points of current occupational status is over 8%. The return to schooling net of experience, social origins, occupational attainments, labor supply, and unionization is about 2%. As others have found (Sewell and Hauser, 1975; Treiman and Hauser, 1977), there is a direct effect of parental income on earnings which is not mediated by schooling, experience, occupational achievements, or labor supply variables. The elasticity of earnings with respect to parental income in the final earnings equation is .046, which is about 40% of its total effect.

The total effect of schooling appears to be overstated by about 7% when social origins are excluded from the earnings function, and social origins make a negligible contribution to the variation in earnings net of schooling and experience (cf. lines 2 and 7). Finally, experience has a suppressor effect on the total return to schooling. Experience and schooling both enhance earnings, but the two are negatively correlated. Schooling and work are alternative uses of the time of individuals so, within a birth cohort, men with more schooling will have less work experience. Moreover, men in older cohorts, who have more experience, obtained less schooling in the aggregate than more recent cohorts. Thus the ED coefficient is almost 30% lower in line 8 than in line 7 of Table 9.

Table 10 presents structural and reduced forms of the same earnings function estimated from uncorrected CPS-OCGQ full-sample moments. Comparing corresponding estimates in Tables 9 and 10 allows us to assess the apparent bias in the uncorrected estimates, assuming response errors are mutually uncorrelated.

First, we note that the total variation in earnings, σ_t, is overstated by about 4% when response errors are ignored. Residual variation, σ_u, which includes measurement errors in reports of earnings in the uncorrected estimates in Table 10, is overestimated 5% to 9% in the reduced-form equations (lines 1 to 5), and 11% in the structural equation (line 6). Thus, if we ignore response errors, we slightly overstate the total amount of earnings inequality which *cannot* be attributed to the factors represented in our earnings function. (The biases in estimates of unexplained variation were much higher, up to 27%, in equations for educational and occupational attainments; see Bielby et al., 1977a.) The amount of variation in earnings attributable to the variables in the earnings function, explained variation $\sigma_{\hat{t}}$, is underestimated by no more than

TABLE 10

Uncorrected Estimates of Parameters of an Earnings Function for 1972 Earned Income (LINEARN): Nonblack Males in the Experienced Civilian Labor Force, March 1973, Who Reported at Least $1000 in the Current Population Survey (N=24,352)

Equation	EX	EX2	FO[b]	FE	PI	ED	OI[b]	OC[b]	WKS	FT	UN	R^2	Residual σ_u	Explained σ_t	Total σ_t
													Components of Variation[a]		
1.	.0158 (.326)	-.0119 (-.324)	.0238 (.084)	.0093 (.057)	.103 (.146)	--	--	--	--	--	--	.160	.599	.261	.6534
2.	.0189 (.389)	-.0111 (-.303)	.0092 (.032)	-.0028 (-.017)	.054 (.077)	.0706 (.330)	--	--	--	--	--	.231	.573	.314	
3.	.0187 (.384)	-.0109 (-.298)	-.0024 (-.008)	-.0018 (-.011)	.054 (.077)	.0421 (.197)	.0606 (.229)	--	--	--	--	.261	.562	.334	
4.	.0165 (.340)	-.0103 (-.282)	-.0073 (-.026)	-.0016 (-.010)	.048 (.068)	.0231 (.108)	.0306 (.116)	.0715 (.274)	--	--	--	.302	.546	.359	
5.	.0133 (.274)	-.0084 (-.230)	-.0027 (-.010)	-.0014 (-.009)	.044 (.062)	.0224 (.105)	.0287 (.109)	.0597 (.229)	.0256 (.329)	--	--	.403	.505	.415	
6.	.0117 (.241)	-.0069 (-.187)	.0009 (.003)	-.0011 (-.007)	.042 (.059)	.0254 (.119)	.0283 (.107)	.0664 (.254)	.0232 (.299)	.734 (.209)	.200 (.141)	.464	.478	.445	
7.	.0185 (.380)	-.0111 (-.302)	--	--	--	.0781 (.364)	--	--	--	--	--	.225	.575	.310	
8.	--	--	--	--	--	.0566 (.264)	--	--	--	--	--	.070	.630	.172	

NOTE: Standardized coefficients appear in parentheses.

a. Components are expressed as standard deviations. The additive decomposition is $\sigma_i^2 = \sigma_t^2 + \sigma_u^2$.

b. Variables expressed in the metric of Duncan SEI scores have been divided by 10 and corresponding coefficients multiplied by 10.

[147]

3% in the reduced-form and structural equations. In all, there is a 12% to 14% understatement of the proportion of variance explained (R^2) in earnings in the reduced-form and structural equations.

The estimated reduced-form effect of one social origin variable, father's education (FE), is actually overestimated by 22% using uncorrected moments (see line 1), but the reduced-form effects of father's occupational status (FO) and parental income (PI) are underestimated by 14% and 12%, respectively. Further, when response errors are ignored, the unmediated effect of parental income is underestimated by 12% to 15% in lines 3 through 5 and by 8% in the structural equation (line 6).

While the total effect of education (ED) is underestimated by 16% (a return of about 7% per year in line 2 of Table 10 and nearly 8.5% in line 2 of Table 9), the effects of education net of current occupation (OC), weeks worked (WKS), full-time employment status (FT), and union membership (UN) are overstated considerably in the uncorrected equations. The unmediated effect of education is overstated by 32% in equation 4, 22% in equation 5, and 18% in equation 6 when we assume errors in reports of education and earnings are uncorrelated.

The total economic return to occupational status of first job after completing schooling (01) is underestimated by 22% in line 3 (a return of about 6% for 10 SEI points in Table 10 and 7.73% in Table 9). However, the net effect of 01 is overstated by about 8% in the structural equation (line 6), and by a bit less than that in line 4. In contrast the total and net effects of occupational status of March 1973 job (OC) are all underestimated by about 20% when measurement errors are ignored.

The total and net effects of weeks worked in 1972 (WKS) are understated slightly in the uncorrected estimates (about 7% in line 5 and 6% in line 6). The effect of full-time employment status is slightly overstated in the structural equation (by about 4%), and the effect of union membership is understated by 9% (despite the fact that both are assumed to be measured perfectly).

The coefficients of the experience variables, EX and EX2, are barely affected by measurement errors. The largest bias is about 6% in the coefficient of EX2 in the structural equation (line 6). The peak of the earnings-experience profile differs at most by about one year in the corrected and uncorrected equations.

The specification bias in the total effect of schooling (ED), when social origin variables are ignored (line 7 versus line 3), actually appears larger when the comparison is made from uncorrected (Table 10) instead of corrected (Table 9) coefficients. The overstatement is about 7%

in Table 9 and 11% in Table 10. This finding, contrary to what Bowles (1972) and others have implied, occurs because social origins are measured about as reliably as educational attainment.

Our findings about bias under the specification of random measurement error may be summarized as follows. The total effects (coefficient of variation in the first equation in which it appears) of two of three social origin variables, FO and PI, and of educational attainment are modestly underestimated (by 12% to 16%) when response errors are ignored. The total effects of occupational attainments, O1 and OC, are underestimated by an even greater amount, over 20%, and the net returns to current occupational status are also underestimated by about 20%. Biases in effects of labor supply variables, WKS and FT, and of union membership are considerably smaller. The return to parental income that is unmediated by other variables is consistently underestimated by 8% to 15%. In contrast, the unmediated effects of schooling are overestimated by as much as 32% when we ignore measurement error. Variation in earnings not attributable to factors represented in the earnings function is overstated by 5% (in the reduced form) and by 11% (in the structural form). Overall, the proportion of variance explained in earnings is underestimated by no more than 13% when random response errors are ignored.

These comparisons have been based on the assumption that there is no negative correlation between response errors of CPS reports of education and earnings. Corrected estimates under the alternate assumption that $\rho_{e_{41},e_{81}} = -.14$ yield estimates that are, for the most part, quite close to the corrected estimates of Table 9, obtained under the assumption that $\rho_{e_{41},e_{81}} = 0$. There is one significant difference under the alternate specification (those estimates are available on request from the authors). The negative error correlation causes an increase in the corrected *net* return to education such that uncorrected, unmediated effects of schooling appear to be *underestimated* 14% to 20%, while the apparent biases in uncorrected returns to parental income (PI) and status of first job (O1) are correspondingly reduced. The results are not surprising, since the negative error correlation implies a larger true covariation between education and earnings than does the random error model. However, the *total* effects of each variable are essentially unchanged. While the ambiguous status of the error correlation confounds our interpretation of the *way* in which schooling confers advantages in the labor market, we are relatively certain that the *total* true return to an additional year of schooling in our earnings function is on the order of 8.5% to 9%, and consequently uncorrected estimates understate the total return to an additional year by 16% to 20%.

To this point we have assumed that the response errors in CPS and ISR earnings reports are uncorrelated. As noted above, our earlier research found no evidence of within-variable error correlation for reports of social origins, educational attainment, or occupational statuses, and it seems reasonable to assume that errors in earnings reports are also uncorrelated. Nevertheless, the correlation between the two reports of earnings is surprisingly high, .94, and it is possible that some contamination in response errors of earnings occurs across measurement occasions. However, it can be shown that the only effects of a positive value of $\rho_{e_{81},e_{82}}$ on the other measurement model parameters are: (1) the error variations of reports of earnings, $\sigma_{e_{81}}$ and $\sigma_{e_{82}}$, increase; (2) the true score variation in earnings decreases; and (3) the error correlations, $\rho_{e_{41},e_{81}}$ and $\rho_{e_{72},e_{82}}$, decrease (without changing the corresponding error covariances). Consequently, the implications for the corrected estimates of the substantive model are: (1) the unexplained component of variation, σ_u, is decreased as error variation increases; (2) corrected metric coefficients in the earnings function are *unchanged*, since true score covariances and true score variances of predetermined variables are unchanged; and (3) standardized coefficients in the earnings function increase in proportion to the ratio of the original and modified standard deviations of true earnings. We found that, even assuming the with-variable error correlation, $\rho_{e_{81},e_{82}}$, to be as high as 0.50 (the value assumed by Bowles, 1972), the affected parameters of both the measurement model and substantive model were altered by only trivial amounts (detailed results are available from the authors on request). Thus, even a substantial within-variable correlation between errors in reports of earnings does not change our overall interpretation of the effects of response error on the parameters of earnings functions.

CONCLUSION

Several sociologists and economists have noted possible biases in effects of social background and schooling when intergenerational models of occupational and economic success are based on retrospective survey reports of status variables. The prevailing view has been that effects of social background are biased downward by errors in retrospective reports; consequently, effects of schooling are biased upward, at least relative to those of social background. But research on these biases has been inconclusive because appropriate data and statistical models have not been available. Using data from the Income Supplement Reinterview program of the March 1973 Current Population Survey and the remeasurement program of the 1973 Occupational Changes in a Generation survey, we have overcome some of these shortcomings by estimating and testing comprehensive structural models which incorporate both random and nonrandom response errors.

Our earlier research presented evidence that the reports of social origins, education, and occupational attainments by nonblack males are subject to only random response error. The results presented here suggest that Current Population Survey reports of weeks worked and earnings are probably also subject to random errors, although conflicting evidence was presented on whether there is a slight tendency for CPS respondents to understate the consistency between their earnings and education. We also detected a tendency for respondents to overstate the consistency between their 1972 earnings and the number of weeks worked in 1972 in their Income Supplement Reinterview responses.

Ignoring response error, we underestimate the effects of two social-origin variables, father's occupational status and parental income, by 14% and 12%, respectively. Contrary to some previous expectations, we also underestimate the total effect of schooling by an even greater amount, 16%, and we detect even larger understatements, more than 20%, in total returns to occupational attainments when measurement errors are ignored. The unmediated effects of parental income and March 1973 occupational status are also moderately understated in uncorrected estimates. We are less certain about the effects of response errors on estimates of the net returns to schooling, unmediated by occupational attainments, labor supply, and/or union membership. If response errors are indeed random, then the unmediated effects of schooling are overestimated by as much as 32% when those errors are ignored. However, if CPS respondents do indeed understate the consistency between their schooling and earnings, then the unmediated effects of schooling are understated by as much as 20%

Overall, we were rather surprised at the relative accuracy with which earnings are reported in the Current Population Survey. Indeed, logarithmic earnings appears to be one of the most accurately measured statuses in social surveys of the type examined here. Consequently, response errors bias estimates of coefficients of an earnings function by no more than they bias estimates for equations representing determinants of educational and occupational attainments. Components of variation in earnings are considerably less affected by response error than are components of variation in schooling and occupational attainments.

Our results failed to confirm the hypothesis of Bowles (1972) and others that because of errors of measurement, estimates of earnings functions substantially overstate the influence of schooling vis-à-vis social origins. The results presented here do *not* directly address whether response errors bias the extent to which the total and net effects of schooling *transmit* inequality in social origins. Our earlier research (Bielby et al., 1977a; 1977b) suggests that the degree to which ignoring measurement error leads to understatement of the transmission of social inequality by schooling is neither trivial nor overwhelming.

In closing, we note that measurement and scaling procedures appear to have substantial effects on the quality of data even where survey methods are highly standardized. Our experiments with scaling earnings show that simple transformation of a measure can greatly affect its quality. The procedures employed to collect data on the four measurement occasions appear systematically related to the reliability of the data. Personal interviews appear to be more accurate than telephone interviews which in turn appear to be more accurate than self-administered questionnaires. Our earlier research (Bielby, 1976; Bielby et al., 1977b) indicated that at least one attribute of the respondent, race, affects considerably the reliability of data obtained from surveys. Finally, our alternate measurement model specification, incorporating the single within-occasion error correlation, demonstrated that if such response effects do indeed exist, they can have substantial effects on estimates of some coefficients in structural equation models. Sound research design demands that all of these factors be given careful attention. We hope that our results, based on data collected from one carefully designed social survey, will aid in the design and analysis of other surveys.

NOTES

1. While our findings for black males were less conclusive, they suggested that the pattern of measurement error for blacks is substantially more complex than the pattern for nonblacks. Comparisons of black and nonblack error structures and their implications for racial differences in the occupational achievement process are presented in Bielby et al. (1977b).

2. The OCG parental income item was: "When you were about 16 years old, what was your family's annual income?" The variable was scaled as the natural logarithm of price-adjusted dollar midpoints of the 14 possible response categories (see Bielby, et al., 1977b: 1248-1249 for further details).

3. The sample person was instructed to report the year in which he actually began the job, even if he started it before completing schooling. Consequently, for some persons our definition includes labor market experience obtained before completion of schooling, and it includes military experience if a person held a full-time civilian job after completing schooling but before entering the military.

Year of first job was not reported for about 11% of the cases. For these cases, the year schooling was completed, if reported, was used to compute labor-market experience. For the remaining 5% of the cases, experience was computed as age - educational attainment - 5. Labor-force experience obtained before 10 years of age was not counted. For less than 1% of the cases, no experience measure was computed, because of inconsistencies between age, educational attainment, and year schooling was completed.

4. Experience and age are correlated .914 in the full CPS-OCGQ sample. Consequently, our results would be quite similar had we controlled year of birth (age) instead of year of entry to first job (experience). The role of age and experience in earnings functions and the appropriate definition of experience have been the subject of considerable debate. For example, see Griffin (forthcoming), Blinder (1976), and Rosenzweig (1976).

5. The term, true score, should be interpreted cautiously. As in the classic psychometric model, the true scores are defined as latent or unobservable variates which underlie repeated observable measurements. For this reason, our findings about the quality of specific measures do not establish their validity in global terms. For example, the true score underlying repeated self-reports of a man's occupation might differ from that underlying repeated reports by his employer. Thus "latent or unobserved variable" is synonymous with true score as we use the term.

6. The two reports (OCGQ and OCGR) of union membership are identical for almost all cases, as are the two reports (CPS and ISR) of full-time employment status. The assumption that work experience is measured perfectly is less tenable. However, the quality of that measure will not be assessed here (but see Bielby, 1976: 112-114). Preliminary models showed slightly larger effects for linear and quadratic age terms than for linear and quadratic experience terms. We surmise that the difference would disappear if we could adjust for the lower reliability of the experience measure, despite the different conceptual bases for the age and experience terms.

7. The Bureau of the Census uses the "hot deck" technique to allocate nonresponses in CPS reports of education, occupation, weeks worked, and earnings, and we treat these allocations as responses. Allocated nonresponses are assigned the observed value of the last case processed with the same attributes on several characteristics (see Ono and Miller, 1969; Spiers et al., 1972; and Spiers and Knott, 1969, for details of the Current Population Survey allocation procedures). To assess the impact of both allocation and nonresponse, we performed parallel analyses to those reported here, excluding all cases with any missing data or allocated responses. Despite the potential for nonrandom error in allocated responses, our "listwise" analyses yielded nearly identical results to those reported here.

8. We noted above that there may have been a tendency for those with more accurate reports of earnings to be selected for the OCGR subsample. If so, the error variance for CPS reports of earnings borrowed from the ISR subsample estimates may be too large. For a given *covariance* among reporting errors, a larger error variance will reduce the *cor-*

relation among the errors. If this is indeed the case, the fourth-stage models may understate error correlations involving the CPS earnings report. On the other hand, when the λ_{ij} are 1.0, as they are for the reports in question, the *covariance* among observable reports of two variables is equal to the covariance among respective true scores plus the covariance among respective error terms, under the measurement model. That is, the covariance among observables generated by the model is *not* affected by the error variances. Model 3B suggests the covariance among e_{41} and e_{81} is modestly large and negative, while according to Model 4B the covariance among error terms is positive but negligible, regardless of the values of the borrowed error variances. Thus the ISR subsample and OCGR subsample estimates do seem to be at odds in their implications about the degree to which respondents understate (or overstate) the consistency between their educational attainments and earnings.

9. The positive correlation between errors in ISR reports of weeks worked and earnings did not disappear in the listwise estimates ($\hat{\rho}_{e_{72},e_{82}} = .14$). Since ISR reports are not used in estimating the earnings function in the full CPS-OCG sample, this error correlation does not affect our assessment of biases due to response errors.

10. Since the CPS report of education is more likely than the OCG report to be a proxy report (provided by the spouse of the designated male), there could be a tendency for 12 years completed to be reported in the CPS when the designated male actually completed slightly more or less than 12 years. Since the mean report is about 12 years, such a tendency would result in a negative correlation between errors and true scores. The ISR subsample shows CPS and OCGQ reports to be about equally reliable, while the OCGR subsample shows the latter to be substantially less reliable. For reasons noted above, the error variation in the OCGQ report is probably overestimated from the OCGQ subsample and underestimated from the ISR subsample.

11. Alternatively, we could have estimated the earnings function directly from the subsamples, or pooled moments from the full sample and both subsamples in order to estimate simultaneously the measurement model and earnings function. The former procedure is certainly less efficient than the one employed here, and we do not know the relative merits and pitfalls of the latter procedure.

12. Under our specification, if b_1 is the coefficient of EX and b_2 is the coefficient of EX2, the partial derivative of earnings with respect to experience is $b_1 + (b_2/5)(EX - 20)$.

REFERENCES

ALEXANDER, K. L., B. K. ECKLAND, and L. J. GRIFFIN (1975) "The Wisconsin model of socioeconomic achievement: a replication." Amer. J. of Sociology 81: 324-342.

BIELBY, W. T. (1976) "Response errors in models of the intergenerational transmission of socioeconomic status." Ph.D. dissertation, University of Wisconsin Madison (unpublished).

———R. M. HAUSER, and D. L. FEATHERMAN (1977a) "Response errors of non-black males in models of the stratification process." J. of the Amer. Stat. Association 72.

————(1977b) "Response errors of black and nonblack males in models of status inheritance and mobility." Amer. J. of Sociology 83: 1242-1288.

BLAU, P. M., and O. D. DUNCAN (1967) The American Occupational Structure. New York: John Wiley.

BLINDER, A. S. (1976) "Dogmatism in human capital theory." J. of Human Resources 11: 8-22.

BOHRNSTEDT, G. W. (1970) "Reliability and validity assessment in attitude measurement," pp. 80-99 in G. F. Summers (ed.) Attitude Measurement. Chiicago: Rand McNally.

BOWLES, S. (1972) "Schooling and inequality from generation to generation." J. of Pol. Economy 80: S219-S251.

————and H. GINTIS (1976) Schooling in Capitalist America. New York: Basic Books.

DUNCAN, O. D. (1961) "A socioeconomic index for all occupations," pp. 109-138 in A. J. Reiss, Jr. (ed.) Occupations and Social Status. New York: Free Press.

————D. L. FEATHERMAN, and B. DUNCAN (1972) Socioeconomic Background and Achievement. New York: Seminar Press.

FEATHERMAN, D. L. (1972) "Achievement orientations and socioeconomic career attainments." Amer. Soc. Rev. 37: 131-143.

————and R. M. HAUSER (1973) "On the measurement of occupation in social surveys." Soc. Methods and Research 2: 239-251.

GRIFFIN, L. J. (forthcoming) "On estimating the economic value of schooling and experience: some issues in conceptualization and measurement." Sociology of Education 50.

HAUSER, R. M. and T. N. DAYMONT (1977) "Schooling, ability and earnings: cross-sectional findings 8 to 14 years after high school graduation." Sociology of Education 50.

JENCKS, C., M. SMITH, H. ACLAND, M. J. BANE, D. COHEN, H. GINTIS, B. HEYNS, and S. MICHELSON (1972) Inequality. New York: Basic Books.

JORESKOG, K. G. (1973) "A general method for estimating a linear structural equation system," pp. 85-112 in A. S. Goldberger and O. D. Duncan (eds.) Structural Equation Models in the Social Sciences. New York: Seminar Press.

————(1970) "A general method for analysis of covariance structures." Biometrika 57: 239-251.

————G. T. GRUVAEUS, and M. van THILLO (1970) "ACOVS: a general computer program for analysis of covariance structures." Princeton: Educational Testing Service: Research Bull. 70-15.

MINCER, J. (1974) Schooling, Experience, and Earnings. New York: National Bureau of Economic Research.

ONO, M. and H. P. MILLER (1969) "Income nonresponses in the current population survey." Proceedings of the Social Statistics Section, 1969. Amer. Stat. Association: 227-288.

ROSENZWEIG, M. R. (1976) "Nonlinear earnings functions, age, and experience: a nondogmatic reply and some additional evidence." J. of Human Resources 11: 23-27.

SEWELL, W. H. and R. M. HAUSER (1975) Education, Occupation and Earnings: Achievement in the Early Career. New York: Academic Press.

SIEGEL, P. M. and R. W. HODGE (1968) "A causal approach to the study of measurement error," pp. 28-59 in H. M. Blalock and A. B. Blalock (eds.) Methodology in Social Research. New York: McGraw-Hill.

SPIERS, E., J. CODER and M. ONO (1972) "Characteristics of income nonrespondents in the current population survey." Proceedings of the Social Statistics Section, 1971. Amer. Stat. Association: 369-374.

SPIERS, E. and J. J. KNOTT (1969) "Computer method to process missing income and work experience information in the current population survey." Proceedings of the Social Statistics Section, 1969. Amer. Stat. Association: 289-297.

TREIMAN, D. J. and R. M. HAUSER (1977) "The intergenerational transmission of income," pp. 271-302 in R. M. Hauser and D. L. Featherman, The Process of Stratification: Trends and Analyses. New York: Academic Press.

WRIGHT, E. O. and L. PERRONE (1977) "Marxist class categories and income inequality." Amer. Soc. Rev. 42: 32-55.

William T. Bielby is Assistant Professor of Sociology at the University of California-Santa Barbara. Currently, he is engaged in research on positional inequality in the American occupational structure.

Robert M. Hauser is Professor of Sociology at the University of Wisconsin. He is working with a colleague on a study of changes in the American system of social stratification and with another colleague on a study of the development of socioeconomic inequality over the life cycle. His forthcoming and recent books include The Process of Stratification: Trends and Analyses *and* Opportunity and Change *(both co-authored with David L. Featherman), and* Schooling and Achievement in American Society *(co-edited with William H. Sewell and David L. Featherman).*